HOW SHOULD THE UNITED STATES WITHDRAW FROM IRAQ?

Neal J. Pozner, *Book Editor*

Bruce Glassman, *Vice President*
Bonnie Szumski, *Publisher*
Helen Cothran, *Managing Editor*

OPPOSING
VIEWPOINTS®
SERIES

GREENHAVEN PRESS

An imprint of Thomson Gale, a part of The Thomson Corporation

THOMSON
—————★—————
GALE

Detroit • New York • San Francisco • San Diego • New Haven, Conn.
Waterville, Maine • London • Munich

THOMSON

GALE

LIBRARY OF CONGRESS CATALOGING-IN-PUBLICATION DATA

How should the United States withdraw from Iraq? / Neal J. Pozner, book editor.
    p. cm. — (At issue)
Includes bibliographical references and index.
ISBN 0-7377-2322-X (lib. : alk. paper) — ISBN 0-7377-2323-8 (pbk. : alk. paper)
    1. Iraq War, 2003. 2. United States—Relations—Iraq. 3. Iraq—Relations—United States. 4. United States—Politics and government—2001– . I. Pozner, Neal J., 1977– . II. At issue (San Diego, Calif.)
DS79.76.S56 2005
956.7044'3—dc22
                                                       2004045563

Printed in the United States of America

Contents

Introduction

The question of whether the United States military should withdraw from Iraq is really a question of when and how. Very few people want to see a perpetual occupation of that country. However, the presence of American military forces in Iraq has proven to be a divisive and controversial issue. Each stage of the conflict, from the question of whether the war was even necessary to how it was conducted, has been subject to fierce debate. Contributing to the debate is the instability of the situation in Iraq, which seems to grow more chaotic the longer the occupation goes on. Decisions about when and how to withdraw from Iraq are sure to invite as much debate as the decision to go to war with Iraq in the first place.

In the wake of the September 11, 2001, terrorist attacks on America, the United States began to focus on the regime of Iraq's dictator, Saddam Hussein, which was thought to possess weapons of mass destruction in violation of UN resolutions. Hussein had been compelled to destroy his stocks of biological and chemical weapons after suffering a defeat in the 1991 Gulf War, but he had never fully cooperated with weapons inspectors from the United Nations. After September 11, the United States became concerned that Hussein, working alone or in concert with a terrorist organization such as al Qaeda, might use such weapons in another attack on America.

Although weapons inspectors from the United Nations were allowed to search Iraq in late 2002 and early 2003, Hussein's regime seemed reluctant to cooperate with them. For example, after claiming they no longer possessed any weapons banned by the 1991 cease-fire agreement, Hussein's government begrudgingly pointed inspectors to a small supply of medium-range missiles buried in the desert. Claiming that Iraq had been allowed to circumvent international law long enough, U.S. president George W. Bush appealed to the UN Security Council for authorization to attack Iraq. The council, however, did not approve a resolution explicitly authorizing the United States to use military force against Iraq if Hussein did not comply with weapons inspectors.

Despite this setback, President Bush swore to attack Iraq with or without the consent of the United Nations. "I have said that if Saddam Hussein does not disarm, we will lead a coalition to disarm him. And I mean it," he told reporters on February 7, 2003. The populace of the United States, meanwhile, was deeply divided on whether a unilateral invasion of Iraq was the proper course of action.

Despite the protests and lack of consensus in the international community, on March 19, 2003, the United States and it allies (primarily Great Britain, Poland, and Spain) launched a massive military assault against Iraq, aimed at toppling the regime of Saddam Hussein. In an address to the nation, Bush alluded once again to the threat Iraq's weapons posed, stating,

The people of the United States and our friends and allies will not live at the mercy of an outlaw regime that threatens the peace with weapons of mass murder. We will meet that threat now, with our Army, Air Force, Navy, Coast Guard and Marines, so that we do not have to meet it later with armies of fire fighters and police and doctors on the streets of our cities.

A military victory over Hussein's government was swiftly achieved, with the U.S. Army capturing the capital city of Baghdad by April 9, 2003. President Bush signaled an end to major combat operations on May 1, 2003, aboard the deck of the aircraft carrier USS *Abraham Lincoln*. The president struck an optimistic tone in his speech, remarking, "The transition from dictatorship to democracy will take time, but it is worth every effort. Our coalition will stay until our work is done. Then we will leave, and we will leave behind a free Iraq."

While most people recognized that Saddam Hussein had been a brutal dictator, they remained troubled by the use of unilateral force by the United States. This concern grew when no chemical or biological weapons were found in the months following the U.S. victory. The United Nations' chief weapons inspector, Hans Blix, complained to CBS News that his team needed more time to thoroughly search Iraq before the war. "I think we were given a bit too short a time. A few more months would have been useful." Blix later said that the Bush administration overinflated intelligence reports it received regarding Iraq's weapons programs. He said, "I think that they were inclined to put exclamation marks where they should have a question mark." America's own weapons inspector, David Kay, concurred with Blix, stating that no weapons of mass destruction had been produced since the end of the Gulf War, despite some modest efforts to do so by Hussein. "I'm personally convinced that there were not large stockpiles of newly produced weapons of mass destruction. We don't find the people, the documents or the physical plants that you would expect to find if the production was going on," Kay said in January 2004. If there were no weapons to be found, critics of the Bush administration said, then the United States had fought the war for illegitimate reasons.

Also alarming to many was the rising tide of violence that hampered rebuilding efforts. Hussein loyalists and other insurgents began a reign of violence that steadily increased. As the occupation continued, Iraqis began to increasingly resent the U.S. presence on their soil. The August 2003 bombing of the UN office in Baghdad, along with the October 2003 destruction of the Red Cross's headquarters in Baghdad by Iraqi insurgents magnified the danger still faced by U.S. troops and made many confront the question of whether America had adequately planned for the postwar period. Senator Ted Kennedy blasted the Bush adminstration, saying "The foundation of our post-war policy was built on a quicksand of false assumptions, and the result has been chaos for the Iraqi people, and continuing mortal danger for our troops." The *New York Times* reported on a troubling rift between the army's top officers and Secretary of Defense Donald Rumsfeld:

In February [2003], the Army chief of staff, Gen. Eric K. Shinseki, estimated that it could take several hundred thousand troops to pacify the country after Mr. Hussein was removed from power, an assessment that Defense Secretary Donald H. Rumsfeld dismissed as grossly inflated. The Army chief, civilian Defense Department officials suggested, did not understand the Bush administration's plan for Iraq and was ill-informed.

As the conflict escalated, it appeared that Shinseki had been correct. America did not appear to have troops stationed in Iraq to keep the peace. Retired four-star general Wesley Clark, at the time running for president as a Democrat, also criticized the Bush administration's postwar strategy. He argued that the lack of sufficient troops and a concrete plan for managing the post-war period suggested a deep ignorance on the part of the Bush administration:

> They didn't have a strategy for what to do after they knocked over the statute of Saddam Hussein. No strategy for success. Now, any serious student of warfare . . . understands that warfare is about—not about the clash of armies, it's about the resulting political changes.

Experts discussed a number of strategies to deal with the chaos, from handing control of Iraq to the United Nations to immediate withdrawal without resolution. Eventually, a multistage plan was developed in November 2003, calling for an interim Iraqi constitution to be developed by March 2004. That document would provide the foundation for an interim Iraqi government that the United States could then grant sovereignty to by June 30, 2004. The drafting of the constitution by the Iraqi Governing Council, a body assembled by the United States, proved to be, like most everything else in Iraq, laborious and controversial. The demographic makeup of Iraq, with three major power blocks (Shiites, Sunnis, and Kurds) that disliked and distrusted each other, made consensus difficult to attain. Shiite Muslims comprise approximately 60 percent of the population in Iraq, but they had long been repressed by Hussein's Sunni government and were now beginning to attain power commensurate with their status as the majority. Naturally, Sunnis and Kurds feared that a Shiite majority would harm their own interests. The Sunnis in particular feared this, as they were not eager to give up the power they held under Saddam Hussein. The Kurds, meanwhile, had enjoyed relative autonomy in northern Iraq following the end of the 1991 Gulf War and were not completely enthusiastic about giving up that independence. Unless a government could be created that most Iraqis agreed on, the nation threatened to devolve into civil war. The Iraqi Governing Council finally ratified an interim constitution on March 8, 2004.

While President Bush hailed this as a positive step in Iraq's progress, stating "This new framework will result in protecting the rights of all Iraqis, and will move the country toward a democratic future," others were not so optimistic. Phyllis Bennis of the Institute for Policy Studies questioned the legitimacy of the document, and of any government established by the Governing Council:

> The new Iraqi constitution lacks legitimacy. It was drafted

under U.S. supervision by a body hand-chosen by the U.S. military occupation authorities, and subject to final approval by the U.S. proconsul, Paul Bremer. Its acceptance by the Iraqi population remains uncertain; its ability to actually set the terms for laws to govern the country during the interim period after June 30 remains unknown; its relevance to any truly independent government created after the interim period remains in doubt.

On June 28, 2004—two days earlier than had been announced—a new Iraqi interim government assumed full sovereignty of the nation. Authorities decided on a surprise early handover to thwart possible insurgent and terrorist attacks on the original June 30 date. Iraq's interim prime minister, Iyad Allawi, declared that the new government's policies would be based on four interrelated objectives: the establishment of security, economic recovery, the development of an independent judicial system, and the advancement of democracy. Allawi also stated that Iraq would continue to need the support of the international community:

> We are placing our trust in international commitments of reconstruction aid and debt forgiveness, as well as assistance with multinational military support until Iraq is ready and able to assume full responsibility for its own security. With these efforts, God willing, Iraq will take its rightful place among the free and prosperous nations of the world.

President Bush, furthermore, explained that the U.S. military "will stay as long as the stability of Iraq requires," in response to questions about the continued presence of American troops in Iraq.

These statements of Bush and Allawi reveal that the handover of sovereignty to Iraq brings no definite answer to the question of whether the U.S. military should withdraw from the nation. The authors in *At Issue: How Should the United States Withdraw from Iraq?* examine the central issues surrounding America's presence in the struggling nation. Even though the interim government has taken over, debates over when and how the United States should withdraw will certainly continue to rage.

1

The United States Must Remain in Iraq to Fight Terrorism

George W. Bush

George W. Bush is the forty-third president of the United States.

Following the terrorist attacks of September 11, 2001, the United States declared war on terror, first toppling the Taliban regime in Afghanistan, which was harboring the terrorist group al Qaeda, then moving to Iraq, where U.S. forces ousted Saddam Hussein's regime. The fight continues in Iraq, where foreign terrorists and those who remain loyal to the old terrorist-sponsoring regime oppose the United States. The United States must stay in Iraq as long as is necessary to bring freedom and hope to a region long gripped by oppression and fear—conditions in which terror thrives. The road ahead in Iraq will be difficult, but the United States will stay the course and bring freedom to a troubled land.

Editor's Note: The following was originally given as a speech on September 7, 2003.

Nearly two years ago [in 2001], following deadly attacks on our country, we began a systematic campaign against terrorism. These months have been a time of new responsibilities, and sacrifice, and national resolve and great progress.

America and a broad coalition acted first in Afghanistan, by destroying the training camps of terror, and removing the regime that harbored [the terrorist group] al Qaeda. In a series of raids and actions around the world, nearly two-thirds of al Qaeda's known leaders have been captured or killed, and we continue on al Qaeda's trail. We have exposed terrorist front groups, seized terrorist accounts, taken new measures to protect our homeland, and uncovered sleeper cells inside the United States. And we acted in Iraq, where the former regime sponsored terror, possessed and

George W. Bush, address to the nation, Washington, DC, September 7, 2003.

used weapons of mass destruction, and for 12 years defied the clear demands of the United Nations Security Council. Our coalition enforced these international demands in one of the swiftest and most humane military campaigns in history.

For a generation leading up to [the terrorist attacks of] September the 11th, 2001, terrorists and their radical allies attacked innocent people in the Middle East and beyond, without facing a sustained and serious response. The terrorists became convinced that free nations were decadent and weak. And they grew bolder, believing that history was on their side. Since America put out the fires of September the 11th, and mourned our dead, and went to war, history has taken a different turn. We have carried the fight to the enemy. We are rolling back the terrorist threat to civilization, not on the fringes of its influence, but at the heart of its power.

Fighting terror

This work continues. In Iraq, we are helping the long suffering people of that country to build a decent and democratic society at the center of the Middle East. Together we are transforming a place of torture chambers and mass graves into a nation of laws and free institutions. This undertaking is difficult and costly—yet worthy of our country, and critical to our security.

The Middle East will either become a place of progress and peace, or it will be an exporter of violence and terror that takes more lives in America and in other free nations. The triumph of democracy and tolerance in Iraq, in Afghanistan and beyond would be a grave setback for international terrorism. The terrorists thrive on the support of tyrants and the resentments of oppressed peoples. When tyrants fall, and resentment gives way to hope, men and women in every culture reject the ideologies of terror, and turn to the pursuits of peace. Everywhere that freedom takes hold, terror will retreat.

Our enemies understand this. They know that a free Iraq will be free of them—free of assassins, and torturers, and secret police. They know that as democracy rises in Iraq, all of their hateful ambitions will fall like the statues of the former dictator [Saddam Hussein]. And that is why, five months after we liberated Iraq, a collection of killers is desperately trying to undermine Iraq's progress and throw the country into chaos.

We are rolling back the terrorist threat to civilization, not on the fringes of its influence, but at the heart of its power.

Some of the attackers are members of the old Saddam regime, who fled the battlefield and now fight in the shadows. Some of the attackers are foreign terrorists, who have come to Iraq to pursue their war on America and other free nations. We cannot be certain to what extent these groups work together. We do know they have a common goal—reclaiming Iraq for tyranny.

Most, but not all, of these killers operate in one area of the country.

The attacks you have heard and read about . . . have occurred predominantly in the central region of Iraq, between Baghdad and Tikrit—Saddam Hussein's former stronghold. The north of Iraq is generally stable and is moving forward with reconstruction and self-government. The same trends are evident in the south, despite recent attacks by terrorist groups.

Though their attacks are localized, the terrorists and Saddam loyalists have done great harm. They have ambushed American and British service members—who stand for freedom and order. They have killed civilian aid workers of the United Nations—who represent the compassion and generosity of the world. They have bombed the Jordanian embassy—the symbol of a peaceful Arab country. And . . . they murdered a respected cleric and over a hundred Muslims at prayer—bombing a holy shrine and a symbol of Islam's peaceful teachings.

This violence is directed not only against our coalition, but against anyone in Iraq who stands for decency, and freedom and progress.

Achieving our goals

There is more at work in these attacks than blind rage. The terrorists have a strategic goal. They want us to leave Iraq before our work is done. They want to shake the will of the civilized world. In the past, the terrorists have cited the examples of Beirut and Somalia, claiming that if you inflict harm on Americans, we will run from a challenge. In this, they are mistaken.

Two years ago, I told the Congress and the country that the war on terror would be a lengthy war, a different kind of war, fought on many fronts in many places. Iraq is now the central front. Enemies of freedom are making a desperate stand there—and there they must be defeated. This will take time and require sacrifice. Yet we will do what is necessary, we will spend what is necessary, to achieve this essential victory in the war on terror, to promote freedom and to make our own nation more secure.

America has done this kind of work before. Following World War II, we lifted up the defeated nations of Japan and Germany, and stood with them as they built representative governments. We committed years and resources to this cause. And that effort has been repaid many times over in three generations of friendship and peace. America today accepts the challenge of helping Iraq in the same spirit—for their sake, and our own.

Three objectives

Our strategy in Iraq has three objectives: destroying the terrorists, enlisting the support of other nations for a free Iraq and helping Iraqis assume responsibility for their own defense and their own future.

First, we are taking direct action against the terrorists in the Iraqi theater, which is the surest way to prevent future attacks on coalition forces and the Iraqi people. We are staying on the offensive, with a series of precise strikes against enemy targets increasingly guided by intelligence given to us by Iraqi citizens.

Since the end of major combat operations, we have conducted raids seizing many caches of enemy weapons and massive amounts of ammunition, and we have captured or killed hundreds of Saddam loyalists and terrorists. So far, of the 55 most wanted former Iraqi leaders, 42 are dead or in custody. We are sending a clear message: anyone who seeks to harm our soldiers can know that our soldiers are hunting for them.

Second, we are committed to expanding international cooperation in the reconstruction and security of Iraq, just as we are in Afghanistan. Our military commanders in Iraq advise me that the current number of American troops—nearly 130,000—is appropriate to their mission. They are joined by over 20,000 service members from 29 other countries. Two multinational divisions, led by the British and the Poles, are serving alongside our forces—and in order to share the burden more broadly, our commanders have requested a third multinational division to serve in Iraq.

Enemies of freedom are making a desperate stand [in Iraq]—and there they must be defeated.

Some countries have requested an explicit authorization of the United Nations Security Council before committing troops to Iraq. I have directed Secretary of State Colin Powell to introduce a new Security Council resolution, which would authorize the creation of a multinational force in Iraq, to be led by America. I recognize that not all of our friends agreed with our decision to enforce the Security Council resolutions and remove Saddam Hussein from power. Yet we cannot let past differences interfere with present duties. Terrorists in Iraq have attacked representatives of the civilized world, and opposing them must be the cause of the civilized world. Members of the United Nations now have an opportunity—and the responsibility—to assume a broader role in assuring that Iraq becomes a free and democratic nation.

Third, we are encouraging the orderly transfer of sovereignty and authority to the Iraqi people. Our coalition came to Iraq as liberators and we will depart as liberators. Right now Iraq has its own Governing Council, comprised of 25 leaders representing Iraq's diverse people. The Governing Council recently appointed cabinet ministers to run government departments. Already more than 90 percent of towns and cities have functioning local governments, which are restoring basic services. We're helping to train civil defense forces to keep order, and an Iraqi police service to enforce the law, a facilities protection service, Iraqi border guards to help secure the borders, and a new Iraqi army. In all these roles, there are now some 60,000 Iraqi citizens under arms, defending the security of their own country, and we are accelerating the training of more.

A new Iraq

Iraq is ready to take the next steps toward self-government. The Security Council resolution we introduce will encourage Iraq's Governing Council to submit a plan and a timetable for the drafting of a constitution and for free elections. From the outset, I have expressed confidence in the ability of the Iraqi people to govern themselves. Now they must rise to the responsibilities of a free people and secure the blessings of their own liberty.

Our strategy in Iraq will require new resources. We have conducted a thorough assessment of our military and reconstruction needs in Iraq, and also in Afghanistan. I will soon submit to Congress a request for $87 billion.[1] The request will cover ongoing military and intelligence operations in Iraq, Afghanistan and elsewhere, which we expect will cost $66 billion over the next year. This budget request will also support our commitment to helping the Iraqi and Afghan people rebuild their own nations, after decades of oppression and mismanagement. We will provide funds to help them improve security. And we will help them to restore basic services, such as electricity and water, and to build new schools, roads, and medical clinics. This effort is essential to the stability of those nations, and therefore, to our own security. Now and in the future, we will support our troops and we will keep our word to the more than 50 million people of Afghanistan and Iraq. . . .

The people of Iraq are emerging from a long trial. For them, there will be no going back to the days of the dictator, to the miseries and humiliation he inflicted on that good country. For the Middle East and the world, there will be no going back to the days of fear, when a brutal and aggressive tyrant possessed terrible weapons. And for America, there will be no going back to the era before September the 11th, 2001—to false comfort in a dangerous world. We have learned that terrorist attacks are not caused by the use of strength; they are invited by the perception of weakness. And the surest way to avoid attacks on our own people is to engage the enemy where he lives and plans. We are fighting that enemy in Iraq and Afghanistan today so that we do not meet him again on our own streets, in our own cities.

Defending freedom

The heaviest burdens in our war on terror fall, as always, on the men and women of our Armed Forces and our intelligence services. They have removed gathering threats to America and our friends, and this nation takes great pride in their incredible achievements. We are grateful for their skill and courage, and for their acts of decency, which have shown America's character to the world. We honor the sacrifice of their families. And we mourn every American who has died so bravely, so far from home.

The Americans who assume great risk overseas understand the great cause they are in. Not long ago I received a letter from a captain in the 3rd Infantry Division in Baghdad. He wrote about his pride in serving a just cause, and about the deep desire of Iraqis for liberty. "I see it," he said, "in the eyes of a hungry people every day here. They are starved for freedom and opportunity." And he concluded, "I just thought you'd like a note from the 'front lines of freedom.'" That Army captain, and all of our men and women serving in the war on terror, are on the front lines of freedom. And I want each of them to know, your country thanks you, and your country supports you.

Fellow citizens: We've been tested these past 24 months, and the dangers have not passed. Yet Americans are responding with courage and confidence. We accept the duties of our generation. We are active and resolute in our own defense. We are serving in freedom's cause—and that is the cause of all mankind.

---

1. Congress did approve this request.

2

The United States Should Withdraw from Iraq as Soon as Possible

Charles V. Pena

Charles V. Pena is director of defense policy studies at the Cato Institute, a nonpartisan public policy research foundation.

The war in Iraq was justified by claims that Iraq possessed weapons of mass destruction and supported terrorists. However, no weapons have been found, and the links between former Iraqi leader Saddam Hussein and the terrorist group al Qaeda are tenuous at best. Now the United States must begin to form an exit strategy. The U.S. military is ill equipped to perform an extended peacekeeping mission, and Iraqi resistance to U.S. presence is growing. Moreover, the United States cannot afford to spend billions of dollars in Iraq indefinitely. A new governing framework must be created for Iraq immediately, and elections must follow shortly. Once a new government is in place in Iraq, the United States should withdraw its forces within six months.

The administration's original argument for invading Iraq was based on Saddam Hussein's alleged possession of WMD [weapons of mass destruction]. Such weapons, or even a weapons program, have yet to be discovered, which has generated considerable debate over whether the administration exaggerated the threat posed by Iraq (in particular, how close Iraq might have been to developing a nuclear weapon). Time and history will tell if the allegations of WMD were true.

But a more important criterion than WMD in determining whether Iraq posed a real threat to U.S. national security was the allegation that Iraq was supporting [terrorist group] al Qaeda. Indeed, proof that the Iraqi regime was complicit in [the terrorist attacks of September 11, 2001] or actively supporting or harboring al Qaeda would have warranted U.S. military action, just as it had been justified against the Taliban regime in Af-

Charles V. Pena, "Bush's National Security Strategy Is a Misnomer," *CATO Policy Analysis*, no. 496, October 30, 2003.

ghanistan. Secretary of State Colin Powell presented evidence at the United Nations connecting al Qaeda operative Abu Mussab al-Zarqawi to the Ansar al-Islam terrorist group operating in northeastern Iraq. But a direct connection between the Saddam Hussein regime and al Qaeda has yet to be established. Indeed, although President [George W.] Bush continues to claim that "there's no question that Saddam Hussein had al Qaeda ties," despite no strong evidence to back up that assertion, he also admits that there is "no evidence that Saddam Hussein was involved with September the 11th."

Even if one is willing to give the administration the benefit of the doubt on both WMD and the connection to al Qaeda, this much should be clear now: if there was previously a threat, that threat has been removed. That being the case, the United States must devise an exit strategy.

A deteriorating situation

From the very beginning of the current U.S. occupation of Iraq there were warning signs that the United States can ill afford to overstay its welcome. Thousands of Muslims, both Shiite and Sunni, protested against the American military presence. U.S. troops, saddled with peacekeeping duties that they are not trained to perform, have fired on crowds and killed civilians in Mosul and Fallujah.

Despite Secretary of Defense Donald Rumsfeld's previous refusal to call the postwar situation in Iraq a guerrilla war, the resistance to the American occupation has since been characterized as "a classic guerrilla-type campaign" by Gen. John P. Abizaid, the commander of U.S. Central Command. And there are signs that resistance to the occupation of Iraq will continue and possibly increase. The following incidents occurred within a span of two weeks:

- The Jordanian embassy in Baghdad was the target of a terrorist car bomb attack that killed 11 and wounded 50 people.
- Unrest in Basra—in the Shia-dominated southern part of the country that has been relatively peaceful—has grown as a result of electricity, fuel, and water shortages.
- The main oil pipeline to Turkey in northern Iraq was bombed, costing the fledgling Iraqi economy an estimated $7 million a week in much-needed oil revenues.
- A major water main in Baghdad was bombed, cutting off water to much of the city.
- A terrorist car bombing of the United Nations headquarters building in Baghdad resulted in at least 20 people killed and more than 100 injured.

Rising costs

As of August 25, 2003, the U.S. death toll after the end of major combat operations equaled that during major combat: 138 deaths, if both hostile and nonhostile casualties are tallied. The number of U.S. troops killed by hostile fire during the war was 115 and the number of those killed since May 1, when President Bush declared an end to major combat operations, stands at 62. Given the current level of violence in Iraq, hostile fire casualties after the end of major combat operations will likely exceed the combat count in a few months' time.[1]

In addition to the human cost, the occupation is costing $3.9 billion a month. And although the administration scoffed at the notion before the war, Paul Bremer (the U.S. civilian administrator in Iraq) has admitted that the cost of reconstructing Iraq could be as much as $100 billion. And President Bush has requested an $87 billion supplemental appropriation for Iraqi military and reconstruction efforts, bringing the total the United States is spending on the war and its aftermath to about $150 billion. The lesson should be clear: the United States must leave Iraq at the earliest possible opportunity.

This much should be clear now: if there was previously a threat [of Iraq using weapons of mass destruction], that threat has been removed.

The United States must avoid a Balkans-style nation-building enterprise in Iraq. In November 1995, President [Bill] Clinton assured the American public that U.S. troops would be in Bosnia for only one year. Nearly eight years later, those troops are still there. Unfortunately, that seems to be the course the administration is taking in Iraq. One senior administration official has spoken of a "generational commitment" to Iraq, much like the one made to transform Germany after World War II. And both neoconservatives and liberal interventionists are supporting a lengthy stay in Iraq.

An exit strategy

Unlike Clinton in Bosnia, Bush has not even set a timetable for how long the United States will stay in Iraq; he has said only that "we will remain in Iraq as long as necessary, and not a day more." According to Lt. Gen. Ricardo Sanchez, commander of coalition forces in Iraq, U.S. forces will be in Iraq for two years at an "absolute minimum" and "probably longer." But if the United States can devise a plan and execute a decisive military victory in less than four weeks, certainly the administration can do a better job of devising and executing a plan for exiting Iraq. Here is a proposed timetable:

• The belatedly appointed Iraqi interim authority (originally slated to be in place at the end of May 2003 but not put in place until mid-July) must create the framework for a newly elected Iraqi government in three months or less. And in doing so, the council must be seen to be representing and acting in the interests of the Iraqi people and not as a puppet of the American authority under Amb. Paul Bremer. Admittedly, the Iraqis will be starting from scratch since they have known nothing except dictatorship and authoritarian rule for more than 40 years. But Turkey—and, to a lesser degree, Afghanistan—provide working models for creating struc-

---

1. As this volume went to press, the number of U.S. troops killed in Iraq had surpassed 1000.

tures for representative government in predominantly Muslim countries.[2]

• Hold elections within the subsequent two or three months. This may seem ambitious, but it took only six months from the Bonn, Germany, meeting, which created a plan for a new Afghan government after the Taliban was deposed, to have Hamid Karzai elected as the new president in Afghanistan. And when the United States ousted the Marxist military council that seized power in Grenada in 1983, free elections were held the following year. A potentially sticky issue is determining who will oversee and verify that the elections in Iraq are free and fair. That would ordinarily be a role for the United Nations, but the United States may be reluctant to involve the UN, given its lack of support for the U.S.-led war. One possible alternative might be the Organization for Security and Cooperation in Europe, which provided monitors for Turkey's parliamentary elections [in 2002].

• Once a new Iraqi government is in place, which according to the prescribed schedule would be within six months, begin withdrawing U.S. military forces. U.S. troops are the finest in the world, but they are neither policemen nor palace guards. And a relatively quick exit is not out of the question; after helping depose dictator Manuel Noriega, the United States handed over the Panama Canal and control of Panama to the new government in a year.

Not perfect, but good enough

Most important, the United States must be willing to live with the result, which is not likely to be a perfect democracy. The temptation—as with all nation-building efforts—will be for the United States to stay on to help the Iraqis get it "right." It is only human nature that the United States will want to bestow upon the Iraqi people the same liberties cherished by Americans. But the U.S. government's first responsibility is to the American public, not the people of Iraq. Liberating Iraq and creating democracy may be a noble purpose, but U.S. national security demands only that whatever government replaces the former regime does not harbor or support terrorists who would do harm to the United States.

Indeed, there is some hope that even an Islamic government would not necessarily be hostile to the United States. In the words of one Iraqi, "We thank the Americans for getting rid of Saddam's regime, but now Iraq must be run by Iraqis." To prevent that gratitude from turning to resentment and hostility, the United States must have the wisdom to leave as quickly as possible. Otherwise, the United States runs the risk of reliving its experience in Lebanon in the 1980s or, worse yet, an American version of the Soviet experience in Afghanistan: Arabs and Muslims from the region could flock to Iraq to expel the American infidel, and the United States could be bogged down in Iraq for years.

2. The Iraqi interim government assumed full sovereignty on June 28, 2004.

3

The Iraqi People Support U.S. Efforts in Iraq

Karl Zinsmeister

Karl Zinsmeister is the editor in chief of the American Enterprise, *published by the American Enterprise Institute, a conservative think tank. Zinsmeister spent much of the Iraq war embedded with the army's 82nd Airborne, and published his experiences in* Boots on the Ground: A Month with the 82nd Airborne in the Battle for Iraq.

Recent surveys conducted in Iraq's major cities reveal that the majority of Iraqis are happy to be rid of Iraqi dictator Saddam Hussein and his Baath Party. In contrast to popular perception in the United States, shaped by an antiwar U.S. media, the Iraqi people are generally moderate and secular in their beliefs, and supportive of America's efforts to rebuild their nation. While Iraqis are optimistic about the future and supportive of the occupation (at least in the short term), the United States must continue to prove its commitment to rebuilding Iraq or risk losing the support of that nation's people.

Editor's Note: The following material was originally presented as congressional testimony before the House Armed Services Committee.

Let me open by stating that the remarks I have for you . . . are built on several bodies of evidence. I am the J.B. Fuqua Fellow at the American Enterprise Institute. I was an embedded reporter during the hot war in Iraq, and have written the first book about the war from an embed, entitled *Boots on the Ground: A Month with the 82nd Airborne in the Battle for Iraq.* I remain in close touch with U.S. soldiers and civilians in Iraq who are temporarily the princes of that land as well as its military guardians. I commissioned and wrote the first scientific poll of ordinary Iraqis, which the magazine I edit carried out during the month of August [2003] in concert with Zogby International.

And I want to talk to you today about ordinary Iraqis.

Every politician is acutely aware of the "silent majority" syndrome.

Karl Zinsmeister, statement before the House Armed Services Committee, Washington, DC, October 29, 2003.

The many skilled elected officials in this room know that mass opinion cannot be accurately judged by listening to squeaky wheels alone. One must look beneath the surface, behind the headlines, at the more glacial forces that underlay the roil of daily events.

It is the massive, often silent, *middle* of Iraqi opinion that I personally am tracking most closely as I observe developments in Iraq. And today I would like to offer my judgment that there is much to be encouraged about in the recent evolution of Iraqi views—particularly the views of the rising Shiite majority.

Inaccurate images

There hasn't been a proper census in Iraq for decades, but according to the best estimates from the CIA, 60–65 percent of all Iraqis are Shiites. Under [Iraqi leader] Saddam Hussein they were horribly treated and politically marginalized, but in any democratic regime the Shia are eventually going to run Iraq. (Very likely in collaboration with the Kurds, who comprise another 20–25 percent of the population and are overtly pro-American.)

The portrayal of the Shiites in the U.S. media has not been very positive. I'll give you a concrete example: Just days after I returned from Iraq [in Spring 2003], the historic million-person Shiite pilgrimmage to Karbala and Najaf—long suppressed by Saddam Hussein—took place. The imagery of this event presented in U.S. reporting was pretty scary: Many of you will remember the much-repeated photographs and video of a number of pilgrims cutting themselves with swords as they walked the route, making a bloody mess. The strong impression of the news coverage was that the Shiites were both religious extremists and unfriendly to American ideals and interests.

> *The Shiites I observed were generally thrilled to be free of Saddam Hussein's yoke, and appreciative of the Americans who had pushed him out.*

I had spent most of my time in Iraq among the Shia, and in my experience neither of those negative characterizations were accurate. The Shiites I observed were generally thrilled to be free of Saddam Hussein's yoke, and appreciative of the Americans who had pushed him out.

It so happens that the security for this Shiite pilgrimage was provided by troopers from the 82nd Airborne whom I know well. Their camp had been right beside the road that the pilgrims trod. So I called up one of the officers on the scene—a smart, frank captain and helicopter pilot named Robin Brown—and asked, "Robin, we're getting all this reporting on fanatical, restive, anti-American Shiites. Did something change dramatically in the few days after I left, or what's going on?"

Somewhat stunned, she reported that the pilgrimmage not only came off without conflict, but had actually turned out to be one of the humanitarian highlights of her time in Iraq. "For three solid days there was this constant river of people," she told me, "and they were singing, honking horns, celebrating. We would watch over the low wall separating our compound from the road, and people would wave to us, laugh, and smile. It was an amazingly festive, peaceful, joyful experience."

A different picture

The media vs. reality disconnect on this important event reinforced my concern that the anecdotal temperature-takings that most Americans were relying on for their assessments of Iraq might be incomplete and misleading. So I went searching for more reliable hard information on the true state of Iraqi opinion. I eventually launched a project to do original survey research for *The American Enterprise*, the magazine I edit. Working with Zogby, we collected data in four different Iraqi cities during the month of August [2003]. It was not easy, but the results are extremely instructive. . . .

I'd like to point out that there have now been four substantial polls conducted in Iraq. In addition to our own *The American Enterprise*/Zogby poll there was one by Gallup in September [2003], one by the well-established British firm YouGOV, and one by an Iraqi academic. Though these efforts varied widely in methodology and geographical coverage, their results are reassuringly congruent. In all of them, the Iraqi public turns out to be surprisingly optimistic, unambiguously glad to be free of Saddam, and quite willing to have U.S. troops stay in their country for a year or more to help them get launched on a new footing.

For instance: two thirds of Iraqis say getting rid of Saddam has been worth any hardships that have resulted. Fully 61 percent have a favorable view of the Governing Council, and by 50 to 14 percent they say it is doing a better job than it was two months ago. An informal *New York Times* street poll of Baghdad residents . . . "showed that about 85 percent felt that safety had increased in the last two months, and 60 percent felt that the Americans were doing a good job." (That, mind you, from residents of the part of the country where the insurgents have been most active. In the vast swathes of the country that have been mostly quiet and stable, security complaints are likely even lower.)

What does all this tell us? It tells us that we are doing much better at winning the hearts and minds of everyday Iraqis than many of us realize.

A moderate Iraq

The survey research we did at *The American Enterprise* reveals that the Iraqi public is not nearly so fanatical, seething, or disgusted with the United States as local extremists would have us believe. Perhaps most interestingly, our evidence suggests that none of the three major nightmare scenarios for Iraq seem likely to come to pass.

First of all, there will be no Baathist revival—Saddam and his cronies are enormously unpopular in the country. Asked by *The American Enterprise* whether Baath Party officials who committed crimes should be punished or whether it would be better to put the past behind us, Iraqis opined vehemently (74 percent to 18 percent) that the Baathists should be punished.

The second nightmare scenario is that al-Qaeda–style [terrorist] organizations would proliferate in the new Iraq. But there is little natural base in Iraq for the jihadist message. For instance, al-Jazeera, the Arab TV network that often serves as a mouthpiece for al-Qaeda leaders, is not popular with Iraqis (who resent its apologism for Saddam's regime). We asked Iraqis what they think of [al-Qaeda leader] Osama bin Laden,[1] and 57 percent of those with an opinion view him unfavorably, with fully 41 percent of them saying their view is *very* unfavorable. As foreign jihadists murder increasing numbers of Iraqi civilians, Iraqi police, and Iraqi popular figures like Ayatollah Hakim, I expect resentment toward al-Qaeda–style groups will grow even wider in the months ahead.

> *In all of [the surveys], the Iraqi public turns out to be surprisingly optimistic, unambiguously glad to be free of Saddam, and quite willing to have U.S. troops stay in their country for a year or more to help them get launched on a new footing.*

The third nightmare scenario that can, I believe, be dispatched is the idea that an Iranian-style theocracy could take hold in Iraq. Iraqis are quite secular—43 percent told us they had not attended Friday prayer even once within the previous month. And when we asked directly whether they would like to have an Islamic government, Iraqis told us "no" by 60 percent to 33 percent.

Interestingly, on all of these questions the majority Shiites fell on the more moderate side. For instance, they are much less likely than other Iraqis to want a theocratic government, are more favorable toward democracy, are more likely to pick the U.S. as the best model for a government, and they are much more unfavorable toward Osama bin Laden.

Signs of stability

I've been further encouraged by very recent signs of maturity and moderation among both the leadership and the rank-and-file of Iraqi Shiites. The first big test came after the murder of Ayatollah Bakr Hakim (and scores of innocent bystanders) outside one of Islam's holiest mosques in Najaf. More than 300,000 mourners attended the funeral in September 2003, which could easily have turned into a rampage against other Iraqis or American troops. Instead, the Shiite faithful showed a willingness to patiently await the official investigation into the crime.

Then [on October 17, 2003] American forces and Iraqi police clamped down on Moktada Sadr, a radical Shiite calling for active resistance against Iraq's existing authorities. Sadr's militiamen had killed Iraqi policemen and American soldiers and forcibly seized government and religious buildings, but coalition forces had moved gingerly against him because of uncertainty as to his popular following. As it turns out, [the] disarming and arrest of Sadr acolytes was actually cheered loudly by other Shiites, who openly repudiated the cleric's radicalism. And the street demonstrations and popular revolt Sadr threatened in response fizzled completely.

---

1. The al-Qaeda terrorist network, led by Osama bin Laden, was responsible for the September 11, 2001, terrorist attacks on the United States.

The very latest bit of evidence of Shiite moderation and willingness to help remake Iraq was the composed reaction of Mouwafak Rabii, a Shiite member of the Iraqi Governing Council, to the bombing of the Red Cross headquarters in Baghdad. He did not rail, or second-guess, but rather urged the United States to speed up American training of Iraqi police and called on U.S. commanders to unleash their troops for more aggressive action against the insurgents.

Extremists in the minority

The relatively small number of extremists conducting murder and sabotage in the Sunni Triangle [where resistence to U.S. presence is strongest] have no chance of winning militarily. Much more than outsiders realize, Iraq's economy and society are beginning to hum. Markets are full, traffic clogs streets, almost all services already exceed their pre-war level, 170 newspapers are being published, schools are well-attended, oil production is approaching 2 million barrels a day, the local democracy councils are functioning surprisingly well and are proving popular. Moreover, the pouncing raids launched in recent months by American soldiers have hurt the guerillas (the bounty paid to induce attacks on U.S. soldiers has reportedly had to be raised from $1,000 to $5,000 to find takers).

The insurgents have no platform, no winning message, no identifiable leaders. There is no evidence that they represent a popular movement, or that they enjoy any widespread support.

Keep in mind, there are now 25,000 soldiers from other countries, plus a healthy 60,000 Iraqi security personnel helping American troops police the country, with many more Iraqi police and soldiers in the pipeline. Even today, just months into a new regime, it is already Iraqis who are bearing most of the casualties involved in guarding and stabilizing the country. Let me note that that will increasingly put the attackers on the wrong side of Iraqi opinion.

The insurgents' only accomplishment is to create chaos. They are strictly a negative force, who can only hope to slow down Iraq's steady climb toward recovery. Finding that they usually die when they fight American soldiers, they have taken to preying mostly on weak and innocent targets like Red Cross buildings, mosques, and humanitarian agencies. This is a desperate and retrograde military strategy that will win them no friends.

The insurgents have no platform, no winning message, no identifiable leaders. There is no evidence that they represent a popular movement, or that they enjoy any widespread support. They instead, are simply well armed and comparatively wealthy fringe fanatics. Many of them are foreign; all of them are leftovers of old Arab power blocs. They are feared by many Iraqis, but not broadly respected, trusted, or liked.

In short, they are political criminals. Everyday Iraqis remember 1991, when America disappeared before the job was done, and many citizens remain wary about acting against political criminals in ways that could put their own lives at risk. But I believe that, increasingly, the guerillas will find it hard to swim and hide among the Iraqi public.

On the side of the angels

The best way to understand our current position in Iraq may be as follows. A psychological contest is under way for Iraqi loyalties. On one side are remnants of an unpopular regime, reinforced by unpopular foreigners, who merely wreck and kill in ugly ways, especially at religious and humanitarian sites, frequently on holy days, with most of the victims being innocent Iraqis.

Iraq is not a bottomless cesspool. It is a manageable challenge.

On the other side are American forces who have, on the whole, been quite gentle and forbearing. (If anything, everyday Iraqis are now more likely to criticize the Americans for being *insufficiently* ruthless in dealing with the insurgents.) And any day now, we hope, those American forces will get a multi-billion dollar infusion of funds—thanks to the U.S. Congress and some of our overseas allies—which will allow them to demonstrate to the Iraqis even more clearly who is on the side of progress, modernity, prosperity, and human decency. And you know what? That's a pretty good position from which to prosecute a war against minority guerillas.

No guerilla war is easy. We will need to strike hard, and to spend money. Improving our intelligence, and training more and more Iraqi compatriots who will fight next to us, and increasingly instead of us, should be high priorities. But there is no Ho Chi Minh trail pumping fresh poison into Iraq, and with each passing season there will be fewer weapons in the hands of fewer guerillas with less and less money to spend.

And, meanwhile, new economic and political freedoms will be unfolding across the countryside—cell phones today, open elections tomorrow. These innovations will cumulatively amount to a social, economic, and political revolution, and make the blood-feuding insurgents look more unattractive to normal Iraqis with each passing week.

A winnable scenario

The one factor that could derail Iraq's gradual rise would be American panic. The Baghdad bombers are not so much trying to influence Iraqis as to cow the U.S. public and stampede our leaders. If we will be long-sighted and steely, we will realize that there is no reason for alarm. The number of our soldiers killed in combat since U.S. forces swept across Iraq in May [2003] is less than the number of police officers killed in the U.S. this year guarding our own streets. All of those men are heroes to their country, but their numbers are blessedly minuscule compared to almost any earlier war, never mind one of this historical significance.

I can tell you the view on this subject of the American soldiers in Iraq whom I know well. They believe this job needs to be finished bravely and without waffling. As one fighter in the 82nd Airborne wrote me . . . : "We are doing great work. We must show the world that we have the stomach for the ugly realities of a righteous war. I believe with all my heart that this effort is critical to the survival of this region, the position of the U.S. as a world leader, and the spirit of our fighting forces in the future. The only way we can lose this war is if we lose our resolve. SPC Babin, who remains hospitalized with brain and internal damage, SPC Bermanis, who has lost three limbs, or SPC Ross, who lost his eyesight and leg saving a young Iraqi, would never forgive us for giving anything less than our all from now on."

My message today is simple: Iraq is not a bottomless cesspool. It is a manageable challenge. The mass of citizens living along the Tigris-Euphrates valley show clear signs that they will make sensible use of their new freedom if we will help them by gradually eliminating the small number of militants conducting murder and sabotage in their midst. In one of the most benighted parts of the globe we are making headway. If we will persevere, future generations will marvel at the American soldiers and political leaders who showed the wit and stamina to turn around a part of the world that has, for more than a generation up until now, been little more than a source of heartbreak.

4

The Iraqi People Oppose U.S. Efforts in Iraq

Robert Fisk

Robert Fisk is the Middle East correspondent for the Independent, *a newspaper published in the United Kingdom.*

The U.S. military treats the Iraqi people as enemies. This results in a growing disregard for the Iraqi people. Indeed, complaints that American soldiers are murdering Iraqis go uninvestigated. Instead of getting to know and understand the Iraqi people, the Coalition Provisional Authority insulated itself from them. In consequence, the Iraqis feel resentment toward their "liberators."

In the Pentagon, they've been re-showing Gillo Pontecorvo's terrifying 1965 film of the French war in Algeria. *The Battle of Algiers*, in black and white, showed what happened to both the guerrillas of the FLN [the Algerian rebel army] and the French army when their war turned dirty. Torture, assassination, booby-trap bombs, secret executions. As the *New York Times* revealed, the fliers sent out to the Pentagon brass to watch this magnificent, painful film began with the words: "How to win a battle against terrorism and lose the war of ideas. . . ." But the Americans didn't need to watch *The Battle of Algiers*.

They've already committed many of the French mistakes in Iraq, and the guerrillas of Iraq are well into the blood tide of the old FLN. Sixteen demonstrators killed in Fallujah? Forget it. Twelve gunned down by the Americans in Mosul? Old news. Ten Iraqi policemen shot by US troops outside Fallujah? "No information," the occupation authorities told us. . . . No information? The Jordanian embassy bombing? The bombing of the UN headquarters? Or Najaf with its 126 dead? Forget it. Things are improving in Iraq. There's been 24-hour electricity for three days now and—until two US soldiers were killed on [September 12, 2003]—there had been five days without an American death.

That's how the French used to report the news from Algeria. What you don't know doesn't worry you. Which is why, in Iraq, there are thousands of incidents of violence that never get reported; attacks on Americans that

Robert Fisk, "Secret Slaughter by Night, Lies and Blind Eyes by Day," *The Independent on Sunday*, September 14, 2003, pp. 20–21. Copyright © 2003 by Independent Newspapers (UK), Limited. Reproduced by permission.

cost civilian lives are not even recorded by the occupation authority press officers unless they involve loss of life among "coalition forces". Go to the mortuaries of Iraq's cities and it's clear that a slaughter occurs each night. Occupation powers insist that journalists obtain clearance to visit hospitals—it can take a week to get the right papers, if at all, so goodbye to statistics—but the figures coming from senior doctors tell their own story.

The Iraqi dead

In Baghdad, up to 70 corpses—of Iraqis killed by gunfire—are brought to the mortuaries each day. In Najaf, for example, the cemetery authorities record the arrival of the bodies of up to 20 victims of violence a day. Some of the dead were killed in family feuds, in looting, or revenge killings. Others have been gunned down by US troops at checkpoints or in the increasingly vicious "raids" carried out by American forces in the suburbs of Baghdad and the Sunni cities to the north. . . . Reporters covering the killing of the Fallujah policemen were astonished to see badly wounded children suddenly arriving at the hospital, all shot—according to their families—by an American tank which had opened up at a palm grove outside the town. As usual, the occupation authorities had "no information" on the incident.

It's as if the denizens of Mr Bremer's chandeliered chambers do not regard Iraq as a real country, a place of tragedy and despair whose "liberated" people increasingly blame their "liberators" for their misery.

But if you count the Najaf dead as typical of just two or three other major cities, and if you add on the daily Baghdad death toll and multiply by seven, almost 1,000 Iraqi civilians are being killed every week—and that may well be a conservative figure. Somewhere in the cavernous marble halls of proconsul Paul Bremer's palace on the Tigris, someone must be calculating these awful statistics. But of course, the Americans are not telling us. it's like listening to Iraq's American-run radio station. Death—unless it's on a spectacular scale like the Jordanian or UN or Najaf bombings—simply doesn't get on the air. Even the killing of American troops isn't reported for 24 hours. Driving the highways of Iraq, I've been reduced to listening to the only radio station with up-to-date news on the guerrilla war in Iraq: Iran's "Alam Radio", broadcasting in Arabic from Tehran.

American attitudes

It's as if the denizens of Mr Bremer's[1] chandeliered chambers do not regard Iraq as a real country, a place of tragedy and despair whose "liberated" people increasingly blame their "liberators" for their misery. Even when US troops on a raid in Mansour [in August 2003] ran amok and gunned down up to

---

1. This is a reference to Paul Bremer, the U.S. administrator who led the Coalition Provisional Authority (CPA). The CPA ceased to exist on June 28, 2004, when an interim Iraqi government assumed sovereignty.

eight civilians—including a 14-year-old boy—the best the Americans could do was to say that they were "enquiring" into the incident. Not, as one US colonel quickly pointed out to us, that this meant a formal enquiry. Just a few questions here and there. And of course the killings were soon forgotten.

What is happening inside the US occupation army is almost as much a mystery as the nightly cull of civilians. My old friend Tom Friedman, in a break from his role as messianic commentator for the *New York Times*, put his finger on the problem when—arranging a meeting with an occupation official—he reported asking an American soldier at a bridge checkpoint for his location. "The enemy side of the bridge," came the reply.

With powerful irony, [al-Qa'ida leader] Osama bin Laden's ominous 11 September [2003] tape suggests that he is as anxious to get his men into Iraq as the Americans are to believe that they are already there.

Enemy. That's how the French came to see every native Algerian. Talk to the soldiers in the streets here in Baghdad and they use obscene language—in between heartfelt demands to "go home"—about the people they were supposedly rescuing from [Iraqi leader] Saddam Hussein. A Polish journalist in Karbala saw just how easily human contact can break down. "The American guards are greeting passers-by with a loud 'Salaam aleikum' [peace be with you]. Some young Iraqi boys with a donkey and cart say something in Arabic and suddenly, together, they run their fingers across their throats.

"Motherfucker!" shout the Marines, before their translator explains to them that the boys are just expressing their happiness at the death of Saddam Hussein's sons. . . . Though light years from the atrocities of Saddam's security forces, the US military here is turning out to be as badly disciplined and brutal as the Israeli army in the West Bank and Gaza Strip. Its "recon-by-fire", its lethal raids into civilian homes, its shooting of demonstrators and children during fire-fights, its destruction of houses, its imprisonment of thousands of Iraqis without trial or contact with their families, its refusal to investigate killings, its harassment—and killing—of journalists, its constant refrain that it has "no information" about bloody incidents which it must know all too much about, are sounding like an echo-chamber of the Israeli army.

Poor intelligence

Worse still, their intelligence information is still as warped by ideology as was the illegal Anglo-American invasion of Iraq. Having failed to receive the welcome deserved of "liberators", the Americans have to convince themselves that their tormentors—save for the famous Saddam "remnants"—cannot be Iraqis at all. They must be members of "al-Qa'ida", Islamists arriving from Iran, Syria, Saudi Arabia, Afghanistan, Pakistan. . . . Among its 1,000 "security" prisoners at Baghdad airport—the total number of detainees held without trial in Iraq is around 5,500—about 200 are said to be "foreigners". But in many cases, US intelligence cannot even discover their nationalities and some may well have been in Iraq since Saddam invited Arabs to defend Baghdad before the invasion.

In reality, no one has produced a shred of evidence al-Qa'ida men are streaming into the country. Not a single sighting has been reported of these mysterious men, save for the presence of armed Iranians outside the shrines of Najaf after [August 2003's] bombing. Yet President [George W.] Bush and [Secretary of Defense] Donald Rumsfeld have talked up their supposed presence to the point where the usual right-wing columnists in the US press and then reporters in general write of them as a proven fact. With powerful irony, [al-Qa'ida leader] Osama bin Laden's ominous 11 September [2003] tape suggests that he is as anxious to get his men into Iraq as the Americans are to believe that they are already there.

In practice, fantasy takes over from reality. Thus while the Americans can claim they are being assaulted by "foreigners"—the infamous men of evil against whom Mr Bush is fighting his "war on terror"—they can equally suggest that the suicide bombing of the UN headquarters in Baghdad was the work of the Iraqi security guards whom the UN had kept on from the Saddam regime. Whatever the truth of this—and the suicidal expertise of the UN attack might suggest a combination of both Baathists and Islamists—the message was simple enough: Americans are attacked by "international terrorists" but the wimps of the UN are attacked by the same Iraqi killers they helped to protect through so many years of sanction-busting.

There are foreign men and women aplenty in Baghdad—Americans and Britons prominent among them—who work hard to bring about the false promises uttered by Messrs Bush and [British prime minister Tony] Blair to create a decent, democratic Iraqi society. One of them is Chris Woolford, whose account of life in Bremer's marble palace appeared only in the internal newsletter of the UK regulatory Office of Telecommunications, for whom he normally works. Mr Woolford insists that there are signs of hope in Iraq—the payment of emergency salaries to civil servants, for example, and the reopening of schools and administrative offices.

Insulated from reality

But it's worth recording at length his revealing description of life under Bremer. "Life in Baghdad can only be described as bizarre," he writes. "We are based within a huge compound . . . in Sadam (sic) Hussein's former Presidential Palace. The place is awash with vast marble ballrooms, conference rooms (now used as a dining room), a chapel (with murals of Scud missiles) and hundreds of function rooms with ornate chandeliers which were probably great for entertaining but which function less well as offices and dormitories. . . . I work in the 'Ministries' wing of the palace in the Ministry of Transport and Communications. Within this wing, each door along the corridor represents a separate ministry; next door to us, for example, is the Ministry of Health and directly across the corridor is the Finance Ministry. Behind each door military and civilian coalition members (mainly American with the odd Brit dotted about) are beavering away trying to sort out the economic, social and political issues currently facing Iraq. The work is undoubtedly for a good cause but it cannot but help feel strange as our contact with the outside world—the real Iraq—is so limited." Mr Woolford describes how meetings with his Iraqi counterparts are difficult to arrange and, besides, "key decisions are still very much taken behind the closed doors of the CPA (the Coalition Provisional Authority), or for the most significant decisions, back in Washington DC". So much, then, for the interim council and the appointed Iraqi "government" that supposedly represents the forthcoming "democracy" of Iraq. As for contacting his Iraqi counterparts, Mr Woolford admits that Iraqi officials are sometimes asked to "stand outside in their garden between 7pm and 8pm so that we can ring them on satellite phones"—a process that is followed by the departure of CPA staff for their meeting with "bullet-proof vests and machine-gun mounted Humvees (a sort of beefed-up American Jeep) both in front and behind our own four-wheel drive. . . ." Thus are America and Britain attempting to "reconstruct" a broken land that is now the scene of an increasingly cruel guerrilla war. But there is a pervading feeling— among Iraqis as well as journalists covering this conflict—that something is wrong with our Western response to New Iraq. Our lives are more valuable than their lives. The "terrible toll" of the summer months—a phrase from a *New York Times* news report . . . —referred only to the deaths of Western soldiers.

What is becoming apparent is that we don't really care about the Iraqis. We may think we want to bring them democracy but, on an individual level, we don't care very much about them or their lives. We liberated them. They should be grateful to us. If they die now, well, no one said democracy was easy.

Donald Rumsfeld—who raged away about weapons of mass destruction before the invasion—now admits he didn't even discuss WMD with David Kay, the head of the US-led team looking for these mythical weapons, on his recent visit to Baghdad. Of course not. Because they don't exist. Mr Rumsfeld is equally silent about the civilian death toll here. It's the followers of his nemesis Bin Laden that now have to be publicised.

Bin Laden must be grateful. So must the Palestinians. In the refugee camps of Lebanon . . . , they were talking of the events in Iraq as a form of encouragement. "If Israel's superpower ally can be humbled by Arabs," a Palestinian official explained to me in one of the Beirut camps, "why should we give up our struggle against the Israelis who cannot be as efficient soldiers as the Americans?" That's the lesson the Algerians drew when they saw France's mighty army reduced to surrender at Dien Bien Phu [in Vietnam]. The French, like the Americans, had succeeded in murdering or "liquidating" many of the Algerians who might have negotiated a ceasefire with them. The search for an interlocuteur valable [someone to have a conversation or negotiation with] was one of [French president Charles] de Gaulle's most difficult tasks when he decided to leave Algeria. But what will the Americans do? Their interlocuteur valable might have been the United Nations. But now the UN has been struck off as a negotiator by the suicide bombing in Baghdad. And the Bin Ladens and the adherents of the Wahabi sect are not interested in negotiations of any kind. Mr Bush declared "war without end". And it looks as though Iraqis—along with ourselves—are going to be its principal victims.

5

Americans Support Continued U.S. Efforts in Iraq

Lawrence F. Kaplan

Lawrence F. Kaplan is a senior editor at the New Republic, *where he writes about U.S. foreign policy and international issues.*

Surveys reveal that the American people support continued U.S. presence in Iraq. Indeed, according to studies, the public at large will tolerate higher numbers of casualties than will politicians and the military so long as the public believes that the national interest is being served. Polling data from past conflicts, such as those in Somalia and Vietnam, bear this out. If President George W. Bush can convince the public that the national interest is being served in Iraq, and that progress is being made in restoring order and installing democracy, people will accept the costs of rebuilding Iraq, both in lives and dollars. Support will waver, however, if progress is not apparent.

Incidents like [the August 19, 2003] destruction of the U.N. headquarters in Baghdad, combined with the steady drip of American casualties, have prompted many opinion-makers to conclude the American public has had enough. "Those are good kids that we're sending into the shooting gallery called Iraq," noted *New York Times* columnist Bob Herbert, adding that his readers "have to be nursing the sick feeling that each death is a tragic waste, and this conflict is as much a fool's errand as the war in Vietnam." Nor is this reading confined to the op-ed pages. "There are an awful lot of Americans who are kind of sleepless these days," presidential aspirant Howard Dean informed a crowd. . . . "They are sleepless wondering whether their kid is going to be the next to die in Iraq." Complaining that American troops have become targets in Herbert's "shooting gallery," Ted Kennedy wants to know, "How do you console a family by telling them that their son or daughter is a casualty of the postwar period?"

But the casualties generated in Iraq's "shooting gallery" rile the likes of Dean and Herbert more than they do the public at large. Well before the first shot was fired, a mass of polling data suggested the country's willing-

Lawrence F. Kaplan, "Willpower—Why the Public Can Stomach Casualties in Iraq," *The New Republic*, September 8, 2003, p. 19. Copyright © 2003 by The New Republic, Inc. Reproduced by permission.

ness to tolerate battle deaths in Iraq exceeded even the figures predicted in worst-case scenarios. In 1999, a massive opinion survey conducted by Princeton Survey Research Associates for the Triangle Institute for Security Studies (TISS) asked people to name the highest number of American military deaths they would accept in a war to "prevent Iraq from obtaining weapons of mass destruction." The mean response: 29,853. A CBS News/*New York Times* survey [in] October [2002] found that 54 percent of respondents favored military action even in the event of "substantial" American casualties. Despite the failure to locate weapons of mass destruction, the war's bloody aftermath hasn't elicited much of an outcry, either. In the face of mounting casualties, 58 percent of those questioned in a July [2003] *Wall Street Journal*/NBC poll said American troops should stay in Iraq "as long as necessary to complete the process, even if it takes as long as five years." Another poll in July [2003] this one for the *Washington Post* and ABC, found three in four respondents expected significantly more American deaths, yet seven in ten still believed U.S. forces should remain in Iraq "until civil order is restored there, even if that means continued U.S. military casualties." The most recent *Washington Post* survey, taken during the second week in August [2003], shows the number of Americans who support the U.S. presence in Iraq—seven in ten—remains unchanged. Even a *Newsweek* poll taken in the aftermath of [the] U.N. bombing found that 60 percent of respondents support maintaining current force levels in Iraq for more than a year, with twice as many favoring staying ten years or more as supporting immediate withdrawal.

Well before the first shot was fired, a mass of polling data suggested the country's willingness to tolerate battle deaths in Iraq exceeded even the figures predicted in worst-case scenarios.

There is a story behind these numbers. In recent years, the public's unwillingness to tolerate combat deaths has become an article of faith for America's leaders. The first President [George H.W.] Bush justified the decision to halt the Gulf war short of Baghdad on the grounds that doing otherwise would have entailed further American losses. President [Bill] Clinton imbibed the same lesson after the October 1993 slaughter of crack American troops in Somalia, subsequently offering assurances to the public that any military action would endanger as few lives as possible. Clinton-era Chairman of the Joint Chiefs of Staff Hugh Shelton even devised a "Dover Test" for the use of force: "Is the American public prepared for the sight of our most precious resource coming home in flag-draped caskets into Dover Air Force Base?" According to the TISS data, the architects of U.S. foreign policy believe the answer is no. Seventy-eight percent of officers and a nearly identical percentage of their civilian counterparts agreed with the statement: "The American public will rarely tolerate large numbers of U.S. casualties in military operations." America's foes agree as well. Prior to the first Gulf war, [former Iraqi leader] Saddam Hussein insisted that Americans could never tolerate "ten thousand dead in one battle." For his part, [the terrorist] Osama bin Laden boasted that the collapse of U.S. support for the operation in Somalia "convinced us that the Americans are a paper tiger." But those who insisted the American public has no stomach for casualties were wrong then, and they are wrong now. The real challenge for America's leaders will not be convincing the public to stay the course in Iraq. It will be convincing themselves.

What the numbers tell us

The public has long been less fearful of casualties than America's political and military elites assume—and, for that matter, less fearful than the elites themselves. According to polls taken by the American Institute for Public Opinion (AIPO), the level of support for World War II never slipped below 75 percent, even though more than 200,000 Americans had been killed by mid-1945. World War II, of course, was the "good war." But the absence of a correlation between casualties and public support holds true even in more controversial conflicts. Survey data dating back half a century consistently shows that what determines the public's willingness to tolerate casualties has little do with casualties themselves.

Specifically, polls demonstrate that Americans will sustain battle deaths if they think the United States will emerge from a conflict triumphant, if they believe the stakes justify casualties, and if the president makes a case for suffering them. Each of these measures has important implications for the operation in Iraq. "The public is defeat-phobic, not casualty-phobic," Christopher Gelpi and Peter Feaver conclude in their forthcoming book, *Choosing Your Battles: American Civil-Military Relations and the Use of Force*, which culls a mountain of data to prove the point. In Korea, for example, an AIPO survey found that public support for the war in August 1950 was a sturdy 66 percent—despite the death of 5,000 American soldiers in the two-month-old war. By December 1950, however, that number had plummeted to 39 percent. Because of battle deaths? Probably not. Between November 1950, when Chinese forces intervened in the conflict, and the time of that survey, the United States suffered a series of devastating battlefield defeats. A few months later, once U.S. forces halted the Chinese offensive and launched their own, public support climbed—even as the number of American deaths passed the 20,000 mark. A 1994 Rand Corporation study even concluded that the Korea toll "led not to cries to withdraw but to a desire to escalate."

The real challenge for America's leaders will not be convincing the public to stay the course in Iraq. It will be convincing themselves.

Even Vietnam, where the myth of a risk-averse public was born, proves nothing of the kind. There, too, the public's sensitivity to casualties depended on its faith in the eventual success of the mission. And, prior to the Tet Offensive in 1968, that faith remained substantially intact. Despite the more than 10,000 Americans killed by then, numerous opinion polls taken on the eve of Tet found a clear majority favored either continuing or escalating the war. According to a Harris Poll, 31 percent of those surveyed in mid-1967 cited American casualties as the most disturbing feature of the war. But, in the aftermath of Tet, which the media portrayed as a major defeat, "the impact of casualties on support tripled in size," according to Gelpi and Feaver. Within a month, the percentage of those most troubled by American losses rose to 44 percent. Even so, those favoring a withdrawal from Vietnam never comprised a majority before the Nixon administration's decision to "Vietnamize" the war, when withdrawal became official policy.

Keeping the people's support

Moreover, victory isn't the only source of public resolve in the face of battle losses—a fact that has become fairly obvious throughout the past decade. "[W]hen important interests and principles have been at stake, the public has been willing to tolerate rather high casualties," Eric Larson writes in his 1996 book, *Casualties and Consensus: The Historical Role of Casualties in Domestic Support for U.S. Military Operations.* "In short, when we take into account the importance of the perceived benefits, the evidence of a recent decline in the willingness of the public to tolerate casualties appears rather thin."

The point may seem obvious, but members of the public do not pinpoint vital interests by themselves; the president usually does it for them.

The paramount example of this tolerance was the 1991 Gulf war. As John Mueller's book *Policy and Opinion in the Gulf War* shows, American casualty estimates prior to Operation Desert Storm ranged into the tens of thousands. The public was well aware of these figures. A poll taken by the Vietnam Veterans of America Foundation on the eve of the ground war found that 67 percent knew about a Pentagon estimate forecasting 30,000 American deaths. Far from prompting a collapse in support, a Gallup Poll taken during the same period reported that a majority felt the Gulf crisis was worth going to war over, even if that meant up to 40,000 American deaths. Looking back at the polls, Larson details how the public's willingness to incur casualties derived from the promotion of a "number of foreign policy goals or principles in the Gulf that majorities of the public generally thought were very important"—among them, to deter further aggression by Iraq, to prevent Saddam from developing weapons of mass destruction, and to reverse Iraq's occupation of Kuwait.

Needless to say, the first Bush administration tirelessly advertised each of these interests—just as the present Bush administration mounted a p.r. offensive to explain to the country its reasons for going to war in Iraq. The point may seem obvious, but members of the public do not pinpoint vital interests by themselves; the president usually does it for them. Or doesn't. In Lebanon, for example, public support for the U.S. intervention increased after the 1983 bombing of the U.S. Marine barracks in Beirut. But, when President [Ronald] Reagan backed away from the operation, that support evaporated. Similarly, when 18 Rangers were killed in

Mogadishu, NBC, ABC, and CNN polls found that 61, 56, and 55 percent, respectively, favored sending more troops to Somalia. That support, too, disappeared as it became clear the president himself no longer backed the mission. Numbers like these lead the Program on International Policy Attitudes' (PIPA) Steve Kull and Clay Ramsay, writing in the book *Public Opinion and the International Use of Force*, to conclude that "polls show little evidence that the majority of Americans will respond to fatalities by wanting to withdraw U.S. troops immediately and, if anything, are more likely to want to respond assertively." Neither Reagan nor Clinton, however, made use of the public's inclination.

Mistakes of the past

Reagan and Clinton may have been reticent because the group most likely to recoil from casualties happens to be the very elites who attribute the tendency to the public. The TISS survey found that military leaders consistently show less tolerance for casualties than civilian leaders, who, in turn, show less tolerance for casualties than the mass public. (In Iraq, for example, the TISS survey showed the public would tolerate, as a mean figure, 29,853 deaths, civilian elites would tolerate 19,045, and military elites would tolerate 6,016.) Hence, when policymakers use casualties as an excuse for inaction, Gelpi and Feaver argue, "they are either tying their own hands or responding to constraints imposed by the military." Tying their own hands because, among civilian policymakers, assumptions about a battle-shy public and the steep political cost of casualties have been axiomatic ever since Vietnam. The "lessons" of Vietnam have also become canonical among senior officers, who fear that, as in Southeast Asia, they will be the ones blamed for battlefield losses. Nor, in the years since, have skittish commanders-in-chief or generals done anything to relieve that fear. On the contrary, they have instilled in the officer corps a zero defect mentality, under whose terms casualties have become synonymous with failure. During the '90s, for example, the core mission of the Army's European Command was "To Protect and Take Care of the Force."

The habit of advertising our fears as if they were virtues has emboldened the likes of bin Laden, Saddam, and [former Serbian president] Slobodan Milosevic.

All this may seem like proof of heightened moral awareness on the part of America's leaders—and, in the sense that casualty-phobia translates into a greater concern for human life, it surely is. But, in other ways, it has ensnarled the United States in thorny dilemmas to which these same leaders have yet to provide an adequate response. The habit of advertising our fears as if they were virtues has emboldened the likes of bin Laden, Saddam, and [former Serbian president] Slobodan Milosevic. Closer to home, casualty-phobia has confused the military's mission and ethos, which is to defend the nation, not itself. It has also led to operations like Kosovo, in which civilians below paid the bill for orders that kept U.S. bombers safely above an altitude of 15,000 feet, and the 1998 missile attack on a pharmaceutical plant in Sudan, where the availability of risk-free weapons allowed the White House to employ force casually and without due reflection.

"So long as the president is not panicking at the sight of casualties, neither will the public."

Fortunately, the Bush team has begun to jettison the elites' casualty obsession. To be sure, the White House has benefited from a hardening of public resolve in the aftermath of [the terrorist attacks of] September 11, 2001. Before the war began in Afghanistan [to oust the Taliban, which supported terrorists], for example, polls showed large majorities supporting military action even if it meant thousands of American deaths and a war that lasted years. Still, fearing casualties and a repeat of the Soviet misadventure in Afghanistan, Pentagon officials relied too heavily on proxies and air power. But, after the battle of Tora Bora, where the proxy strategy enabled hundreds of Al Qaeda [terrorist] operatives to flee the area, the United States reversed course, putting large numbers of troops on the ground. Nor did the administration bend when its risky thrust toward Baghdad cost the lives of as many as 20 Americans on a single day. Neither, for that matter, has the war's aftermath prompted any public second thoughts from the president. "There are some who feel like, that if they attack us, that we may decide to leave prematurely," Bush said. . . . "They don't understand what they're talking about."

The magic question, of course, is whether the public agrees with the president. The evidence so far suggests that it does. To begin with, unlike [President Richard] Nixon in Vietnam, Reagan in Lebanon, and Clinton pretty much everywhere, the public trusts and approves of Bush's stewardship of postwar Iraq. A CBS News poll taken during the second week of August [2003] found that 57 percent approve of "the way George W. Bush is handling the situation with Iraq," while a *Newsweek* poll, taken after [the U.N.] bombing, put that number at 54 percent. "So long as the president is not panicking at the sight of casualties, neither will the public," says Feaver. Far from panicking, Bush has been criticized for excessive bellicosity—his "bring 'em on" taunt, for example. Perhaps not the wisest choice of words, but Bush's challenge to the Iraqi guerrillas did telegraph a certain resolve. Responding to the attack on the U.N. headquarters compound, he made the point more eloquently. The bombers, Bush said, "are finding that our will cannot be shaken. Whatever the hardships, we will persevere."

Looming dangers

Second, according to the most recent polls, a majority continues to interpret restoring stability in Iraq as a vital national interest. Hence the 58 percent who told the *Wall Street Journal*/NBC survey that American troops should remain in Iraq for "as long as necessary, . . . even if it takes as long as five years" and the 72 percent who told the *Washington Post*/ABC poll that they should stay in Iraq "until civil order is restored there, even if that means continued U.S. military casualties." This, despite the fact that 75 percent of respondents to the *Wall Street Journal*/NBC poll believe that "most of the challenges in Iraq remain ahead." Nor does the public have any illusions about the human cost this will entail. "There is a public perception that we cannot afford to lose in Iraq," says Andrew Krepinevich, the author of an influential book on counter-insurgency strategy and director of the Center for Strategic and Budgetary Assessments, "and the public's tolerance of casualties will be considerably stronger as a result."

Bush's vulnerability comes from the growing number of Americans who see events going the wrong way on the ground. In the most recent CBS News poll, only 45 percent see "the United States in control of events taking place in Iraq"—a figure that has declined from 71 percent in April [2003]. Similarly, 53 percent of respondents to the latest PIPA survey think the "process of rebuilding Iraq is going 'not very well' or 'not at all well.'" These findings do spell trouble for the president. For public willingness to tolerate casualties remains as much a function of success as anything else. And, for the time being at least, poll respondents believe that the United States has yet to achieve it in Iraq.

How exactly, then, does the public measure success in Iraq? Opinion surveys point to America's ability to promote stability and democracy as two key tests. Of course, measuring order is easier than measuring democracy, and, given polls that show the public believes the United States has lost control of events there, it may also be the more important measure. Rampaging mobs, acts of sabotage, incendiary clerics, terrorist bombings—these are the sorts of things Americans can do without on the evening news. And, if the president intends to sustain public support, he will have to see that Iraq does without them as well. Even if that means more money, more troops, and, yes, more casualties.

6

The United States Must Ask Other Nations to Help Rebuild Iraq

John Kerry

John Kerry is a senator from Massachusetts. In 2004 he ran as the Democratic candidate in the presidential election.

Although the United States toppled Saddam Hussein's regime in Iraq, it is now questionable whether it can establish peace and security in that country. Opportunities to share the responsibility and cost of rebuilding Iraq have been missed, leaving the American people to bear the burden alone. The president should ask the United Nations to help in the reconstruction effort, even though such a step would mean sharing authority in Iraq. The United Nations has experience and expertise in rebuilding shattered nations. Other nations must be brought in to help because failure to stabilize Iraq would put at risk the war on terrorism.

Editor's Note: The following was originally given as a speech at the Brookings leadership forum on September 30, 2003.

I begin by asking a simple question: What does it gain America to win a war and potentially lose a peace? [In the spring of 2003] our fighting men and women bravely swept across the battlefields of Iraq. But now, as summer turns to fall, the Bush administration's lack of courageous leadership, its scorn for shared sacrifice, its stubborn dogmatism has put our troops at risk, creating a potential new sanctuary for terrorism and weakening America's leadership in the world. Today our soldiers' lives, the future of Iraq, and the solidarity of free nations are being threatened not by a tin-horn dictator but by a tin-eared administration which insists that it is always right, refuses to admit when it is wrong, and over and over again misleads the American people.

Our country is paying a high price for the Bush failures. The clearest symbol of that price is the target that is on the back of young Americans serving in a distant desert. Today a soldier in Iraq fears getting shot while getting a drink of water. A squad at a checkpoint has to worry about whether or not an old station wagon driving towards them is a mobile bomb. And the price is paid not only in their security and, too often, their lives, but in the erosion of America's international standing, the prospect of a new danger down the road, and an endless drain on our national treasury.

The Bush administration is asking us to pay more and more for its failures—another $87 billion that the American people are being asked to shoulder alone and which America's middle class is being asked to shoulder disproportionately, money that could be used here at home to make health care more affordable, to pay for homeland security, to keep this president's promise to leave no child behind.

The administration's credibility

This is an extraordinary moment for America and for the world. Just as in Vietnam, arrogance and pride stand in the way of common sense and integrity. "If we're an arrogant nation, they'll resent us; if we're a humble nation, but strong, they'll welcome us." Those aren't my words. They're the words of George W. Bush running for president three years ago. . . . How far we have come since then.

The administration is engaged in sleights of hand that masqueraded as policy but were really just rhetorical checkpoints on a predetermined course. They went to the U.N. [United Nations], but they used it as nothing more than a drive-by on the road to war. This may be the most arrogant, deceptive moment in foreign policy in many decades. And America's relationships with foreign governments and American esteem around the world are at an all-time low.

For Americans looking for leadership, for people across the globe looking for inspiration, the White House has become a house of mirrors, where nothing is what it seems and almost everything is other than what the president promised. And the result is not just an administration that has shredded its own credibility, but has left the very veracity of the United States in tatters.

[One hundred and sixty] Mongolians, 43 Estonians, and 83 Filipinos is not a coalition. It is a coverup.

Who will believe the secretary of state when he next shows photographs at the United Nations? Who will trust this president when he next vows to work with the nations of the world to combat common foes like [the terrorist group] al Qaeda, environmental catastrophe, or AIDS? New leadership in the White House is needed more than ever to restore American leadership in the world.

We were told that Iraqis would see us as liberators. But too often they see us as occupiers—something that was predictable—ruling over their country; preventing self-determination, not providing it.

We were told there would be a great international coalition of the willing. But this president's pride has brought us a coalition of the few barely willing to do anything at all—160 Mongolians, 43 Estonians, and 83 Filipinos is not a coalition. It is a coverup.

We were told the American people would not have to bear all the burden of rebuilding Iraq and that allies and the international community would join us in this endeavor. But an isolated America is now left almost alone to pay almost all the costs. In fact, we are paying other countries to do something, almost anything, in order to create the appearance of a coalition. This isn't burden-sharing. . . .

Missed opportunities

Despite all the evasions and explanations, we are now in danger of losing the peace in Iraq because of the arrogance of this president and this administration both before and after the war. It was bad enough to go it alone in the war. It is inexcusable and incomprehensible to go it alone in the peace. In the last year [2003], President Bush has had three decisive opportunities to build an international coalition on the issue of Iraq. And three times he not only failed, he hardly even tried.

The first opportunity came [in the fall of 2002] after Congress authorized the use of force. That authorization sent a strong signal that the president and the Congress were united in holding [Iraqi president] Saddam Hussein accountable for his failures to keep his commitments and his scorn for the world community. It set the stage for the U.N. resolution that finally led him to let U.N. inspectors back into Iraq.

It was also obvious to everyone but the armchair ideologues in the Pentagon that the United States could not and should not undertake the reconstruction of Iraq on its own.

When I voted to give the president the authority to use force, I said arms inspections are "absolutely critical in building international support for our case to the world." That's how you make clear to the world you are contemplating war not for war's sake, but because it may be the ultimate weapons inspection enforcement mechanism.

But the Bush administration, impatient to go into battle, stopped the clock on the inspectors, against the wishes of key members of the Security Council and despite the call of many in Congress who had voted to authorize force as a last resort. Despite his September [2002] promise to the United Nations to "work with the U.N. Security Council to meet our common challenge," President Bush rushed ahead on the basis of what we now know to be dubious, inaccurate, and perhaps manipulated intelligence—intelligence which the inspectors could have vetted and corrected.

So the first chance for a true international response was lost in a relentless march to war.

There was a second opportunity. After the Iraqi people pulled down Saddam Hussein's statue in Baghdad, American and British forces had prevailed on the ground and it was time to win the peace. It was also obvious to everyone but the armchair ideologues in the Pentagon that the United States could not and should not undertake the reconstruction of Iraq on its own. To do so risked turning a military victory that promised liberation into an unwanted occupation by a foreign and Western power.

From the moment that statue fell, the successful reconstruction of Iraq and the creation of a new Iraqi government depended on the legitimacy of the process in the eyes of the Iraqi people and of the world. And that legitimacy, in turn, has always depended, from day one, on internationalizing the effort. But the Bush administration insisted on a U.N. role that was little more than window dressing. And yet again a critical opportunity was spurned.

The Iraqi people who cheered the fall of Saddam Hussein weren't rejoicing because they thought they had replaced the Republican Guard with the Republican Right.

President Bush's third and most recent moment of opportunity came last week, when he addressed the U.N. General Assembly [on September 23, 2003]. Other nations stood ready to stand with us, to provide troops to help stabilize the security situation and funds to help rebuild Iraq. The president only had to ask correctly. Instead of asking, he lectured. Instead of focusing on reconstruction, his speech was a coldly received exercise in the rhetoric of redemption. [UN secretary-general] Kofi Annan had offered to help several times, but the Bush administration said thank you, but no thank you—and I'm not even sure that they included the thank you. The president was self-satisfied and, frankly, tone-deaf—stiff-arming the U.N., raising the risk for American soldiers and the bill to the American treasury, and reducing ultimately the chances of success within a reasonable period of time and at a reasonable cost.

The president could have gone to the United Nations and owned up to the difficulties that we face, could have put it in its legitimate context for what we sought to do, could have signalled or stated a willingness to abandon unilateral control over reconstruction and governance. Instead, he made America less safe in a speech and in conduct that pushed other nations away, rather than invited them in.

Too high a cost

That failure, I respectfully suggest, will cost us dearly in the months ahead in an Iraq consumed with suspicion, resentment, and continued violence.

Now ultimately, or any day, the administration may well catch Saddam Hussein.[1] We may even succeed in winning a measure of stability. But the question must be asked, at what cost? What will happen to the larger goals, like ensuring that Iraq does not descend into chaos and become a breeding ground for terrorism? How many more lives will be lost because an administration imprisoned by its pride will not admit mis-

1. Saddam Hussein was captured by U.S. forces on December 17, 2003.

takes and change direction? We cannot allow that to happen.

The failure to plan for the post-war has already lost lives and dollars. And the failure is compounded every day by an administration divided against itself. While President Bush may have declared the war in Iraq over, the war over Iraq—inside his administration—rages on. Our troops are not just caught in the danger of snipers and bombs in Iraq, but they are caught in the cross-fire of an administration sniping at itself. The State Department and Defense Department are constantly in conflict over post-war plans. An administration at war with itself, I say to you, cannot win the peace, and certainly cannot do so as effectively as possible.

[In September 2003] it was revealed that Secretary [Donald] Rumsfeld prevented Secretary [Colin] Powell from sending State Department experts to Iraq because, in Rumsfeld's view, they might not be sufficiently anti–United Nations. Medical doctors were vetted to make sure that they were anti-choice. [Richard] Haliburton and other special interests with friends in high places are getting no-bid contracts, and big-time Republican lobbyists are setting up offices in Baghdad to line their pockets with the money that the American people are spending to protect our troops and rebuild Iraq. The Iraqi people who cheered the fall of Saddam Hussein weren't rejoicing because they thought they had replaced the Republican Guard with the Republican Right.

Growing dangers

This administration's brazen go-it-alone policy has placed our soldiers at needless risk and our hopes for success in jeopardy. It has given al Qaeda an opening in Iraq. And it has made Iraq a recruiting poster for terrorists of the future. It has undermined America's legitimacy with our own people, with allies abroad, and it has left them wondering—the Iraqis—when they will get their country back.

For months, there have been warnings about Iraq's stockpile of munitions. [In September 2003] the Pentagon assured Americans those weapons were secure. Today we learn in newspapers across the country that they are not—650,000 tons of ammunition unguarded and uncontrolled.

This administration's arrogance was so deep, they even ignored the warnings of their own CIA experts in Iraq and carelessly disbanded the Iraqi army, resulting in 350,000 angry Iraqis roaming the country without a paycheck, and with guns. . . .

Share the burden

So as we debate the president's request for an additional $87 billion,[2] I believe we need to demand a change in course. The stakes are too high for our troops, for the Iraqi people, for the region, and for the long term of American security; too large to continue down the path of arrogance into a quagmire. I don't believe that we can walk away from Iraq, but we must demand the internationalization of military and civilian operations.

This does not mean removing the United States from the process. It

---

2. Congress did approve $87 billion to fund ongoing military and intelligence operations in Iraq.

does mean inviting others into the rebuilding of Iraq and the rebuilding of its new government. It does mean giving the United Nations a clearly defined role consistent with its capacity and with its experience. Even after the devastating attack on the U.N. compound in Baghdad, I believe U.N. personnel—and U.N. personnel have said it themselves—will return to Iraq if the U.N. is given the proper responsibility and authority.

I don't believe that we can walk away from Iraq, but we must demand the internationalization of military and civilian operations.

We should not abandon our mission, but we must also demand that whatever we spend in Iraq be paid for with shared sacrifice, not deficit dollars. We are already short-changing critical domestic programs—education, health care, homeland security—to pay for George Bush's tax cut for the wealthiest and the most comfortable. Rebuilding Iraq does not have to add to that deficit of dollars and progress. . . .

And all of us must also ask, what is this $87 billion for? Much of it—some $66 billion—is for our troops on the ground. The remaining $21 billion is supposed to be for reconstruction of basic services, such as water, sewer, and electricity, and for training Iraqi security forces. But it also includes $82 million to protect Iraq's 36 miles of coastline, new prisons at a cost of $50,000 per bed, and a witness protection program at a cost of $1 million per family. All of this for a country with the world's second-largest oil reserves. All this while injured American soldiers have been forced to pay for their own hospital meals and National Guardsmen and Reservists are called up without health insurance for them or their families.

If the Bush administration fails to internationalize the effort in Iraq, the American people could see a succession of endless costs down the road. And as we consider the president's request, we must make every effort to ensure the necessary steps to bring both other nations and the United Nations into this operation in a meaningful way, and to transfer the sovereignty to the Iraqi people.

The president's responsibility

The responsibility lies with the president. The Senate can only do so much. But we have a responsibility to do all that we can. We know the dangers that we now face in Iraq—the existing terrorist violence that's verging on guerilla warfare; the increased capacity for ambushes growing, not diminishing; the possibility of Iraq becoming a new version of the old Afghanistan,[3] a protectorate for terrorism; the threat to stability in one of the world's most vital and volatile regions, which grows worse, not better, as this administration persists in its misguided policies. America has a stake in ensuring that we meet these dangers.

The administration's plan will neither win the peace nor keep our

---

3. From 1996 until December 2002, Afghanistan was controlled by a radical Islamist group known as the Taliban. The Taliban provided safe harbor for Osama bin Laden and al Qaeda in Afghanistan.

troops safe. It seems more like Richard Nixon's secret plan for peace that led to more war than it does Harry Truman's Marshall Plan for peace and stability. The issue isn't what we're spending; it's what we're buying.

The American people demand, and I intend to offer, a better plan. It won't be cheap, but it can and must be successful. The cost of failure would simply be too high. To fail in the transition in Iraq, to at least preserve it from being able to be a failed state or a terrorist haven, would put in danger other governments in the region. It would put at risk the war on terror itself. It would send a signal to all in the world that the United States of America is neither capable nor willing to take the risks to live up to what we all know we have to, [after the September 11, 2001, terrorist attacks].

But the administration doesn't have a plan for peace. They just have a price tag. And those who would cut and run don't have a plan either. And the price of abandoning our efforts in Iraq would be every bit as unaffordable. What's needed now is leadership to finish the job in Iraq the right way. With miscalculated arrogance and misleading Americans, President Bush has put our troops in danger and put America in a more dangerous position.

> *If the Bush administration fails to internationalize the effort in Iraq, the American people could see a succession of endless costs down the road.*

But this administration has staked America's reputation and our role in the world on the success in Iraq, and the course to failure is too great. We have to succeed in the smartest, most effective way possible. To build success in Iraq and to bring our troops home, the administration needs to face the truth—abandon its arrogant go-it-alone approach and take these four essential steps at least:

A new plan for success

First, we need a new Security Council resolution to give the United Nations real authority in the rebuilding of Iraq and the development of its new constitution and government, including the absorption of the coalition provisional authority.[4] This shift of authority from the United States to the United Nations is indispensable to securing both troops and financial commitments from other countries.

The Bush administration must stop stonewalling on the central question of control over reconstruction and governance. The United Nations knows how to do this. It's done it before in Namibia, Cambodia, Bosnia, Kosovo, East Timor. Its record may not be perfect, but it is far more experienced in reconstruction and political transitions than the Pentagon. And if the Pentagon were helping in the appropriate way, we would be even stronger.

This is not a mission for soldiers, but for civilians. And putting civilians inside under U.N. authority will enhance the credibility and the le-

4. The Coalition Provisional Authority was eventually dissolved on June 28, 2004.

gitimacy of our effort and encourage other nations to have confidence that it is all right for them to provide much-needed funding and technical assistance.

The U.S. should not act as if Iraq is an American prize of war, but treat it as a nation that belongs to the community of nations. Nor is Iraq the booty of war, with contracts and concessions to be handed out by the administration to favored companies that are less interested in winning the peace than in winning a piece of the pie.

Second, we need a U.N. Security Council resolution authorizing a multinational force under U.S. command, a command that should properly be ours because we are the largest troop presence. We will not put 130,000 American troops under foreign command. But internationalizing the force and placing it under a U.N. umbrella will spread the burden globally, reduce the risks to our soldiers, and remove the specter of American occupation. And the first step of transferring authority is essential to the achievement of the second, and long overdue.

Third, the resolution must include a reasonable plan and a specific timetable for self-government, for transferring political power and the responsibility for reconstruction to the people of Iraq. And it does not have to proceed in the linear form that they have currently defined, which is restricting the capacity to transfer certain obligations to the Iraqis at an earlier stage which gives them some of the empowerment that they need to believe in their own power and the capacity of Iraqis to develop Iraq. Their participation in rebuilding their country and shaping their new institutions is fundamental to the cause of a stable, peaceful, and independent Iraq that contributes to the world instead of threatening it.[5]

Fourth, the administration must accelerate efforts to train and equip Iraqi security forces—border, police, military, civil defense—so that Iraq will have the capacity to provide for its own security over time. And to do this, we will need assistance from our allies and others to train and equip the forces as quickly as possible, to monitor their progress as they take to the field, and to serve as interim security personnel while that process is going on.

Necessary steps

But I emphasize this: Without the first two steps, the involvement of the world by transferring legitimate authority rather than stiff-arming the U.N., you cannot begin to accelerate the pace at the rate that you need to in order to begin to transfer authority and move American soldiers out of harm's way. . . .

We can and we should protect our troops, and we can and should meet our obligations in Iraq. But we should do it in the right way. Failure is no excuse for its own perpetuation. Irresponsibility should not build upon itself. America can and must do better, and I hope that in these critical days ahead we will make the choice to do so.

---

5. An Iraqi interim government was formally established on June 28, 2004.

7

The United States Should Not Ask Other Nations to Help Rebuild Iraq

Reuel Marc Gerecht

Reuel Marc Gerecht is a resident fellow at the American Enterprise Institute, a conservative think tank. He researches issues related to intelligence, the Middle East, Central Asia, and the former Soviet Union. Formerly, Gerecht analyzed Middle East issues for the Central Intelligence Agency.

Politicians from both the Democratic and Republican parties are increasingly calling for foreign troops to be deployed under a United Nations banner in Iraq, although for different reasons. Democrats believe doing so will lend international legitimacy to U.S. efforts in Iraq while Republicans hope that foreign troops will ease the U.S. military's burden. Both parties are wrong. The United Nations is despised in Iraq for a variety of reasons, and foreign troops, particularly those from other Middle Eastern nations, would be met with resistance. Calling on other nations to help stabilize Iraq will only derail the rebuilding effort.

In the Democratic and Republican stampede to find foreign troops to join American GIs in Iraq, virtually no regard has been paid to whether the deployment of these soldiers is wise given the history, culture, and prejudices of the Iraqi people. Both Secretary of State Colin Powell and Defense Secretary Donald Rumsfeld seem to believe that the United States and Iraq would be much better off if a wide array of foreign soldiers—especially Muslims from such countries as Turkey, Morocco, Egypt, Pakistan, and Bangladesh—backed up American GIs. Secretary Powell's views, of course, have been quite constant. He has essentially mirrored the opinion of the Democratic foreign-policy elite, which shares, on most issues, the preferences and reflexes of the foreign service.

This professional foreign-policy crowd wants to internationalize the conflict because liberal internationalists define success first and foremost through an institutionalized multilateral process. Consensus-building for them is in itself a moral good. Their generally Eurocentric lib-left disposition also makes it difficult for them to see success in any undertaking that seriously distances the western Europeans from Americans, as have both of America's Iraq wars. The truths that [al Qaeda leader] Osama bin Laden articulated in his manifestos—that America under [former President Bill] Clinton had been, in the holy warriors' eyes, afraid and in retreat—understandably do not sit happily with Democrats. They'd much rather believe that American assertiveness and unilateralism provoke ill will. Most of the Democratic foreign-policy elite would have instinctively inclined toward the Brazilian U.N. diplomat Sergio Vieira de Mello when he remarked, a few days before he was slain by a suicide-bomber, that the Iraqi people viewed the United Nations positively, but not the Americans.

Misguided theories

Foreign troops in Iraq will, the Democrats fervently hope, give us "cover" from increasing Iraqi violence and discontent. They will make an American occupation of Iraq seem more legitimate to the world and, ipso facto, more legitimate to Iraqis. International cooperation is thus pragmatically and spiritually the only way out for America in Iraq and elsewhere in the Middle East.

What the right believes about Iraq and foreign troops is much less intellectually consistent and generated more by panic. The recent bombings in Baghdad and Najaf have convulsed the Defense Department and the White House. Slowly but surely, the U.S. military and its civilian leadership have begun to contemplate an ugly possible truth: that most Iraqi Arab Sunnis, who were the power base for Saddam Hussein's rule, don't want to let go of Sunni domination of Iraqi society. It had been hoped in Washington that Arab Sunnis, who, after all, had also suffered under Saddam's totalitarianism, wouldn't actively support former Baathists and other potentially violent anti-American forces.

Foreign troops in Iraq will, the Democrats fervently hope, give us "cover" from increasing Iraqi violence and discontent.

However, it appears that Arab Sunnis in Iraq have not collectively and in decisive numbers rejected the past and embraced a nonviolent path to some kind of democratic order—as have the vast majority of Kurds and Shiites.[1] An increasingly sophisticated insurgency by these anti-American Sunni forces seems to be under way. This insurgency may prove short-lived; it certainly will if an overwhelming majority of Iraqi Sunnis reject the violence of the Baathists, the native jihadists, and the foreign holy warriors crossing the Syrian and Iranian borders. Hundreds of foreign

---

1. Iraq's population is comprised of three major groups, the Shiites, the Sunni, and the Kurds. The Shiites are the majority population, although they were brutally oppressed along with the Kurds during Saddam Hussein's regime. Saddam Hussein himself is a Sunni.

holy warriors couldn't clandestinely live for long in Iraq's Sunni belt without a significant number of the surrounding population acquiescing to their presence. One of the main reasons why these same foreign holy warriors have not been crossing the Iran/Iraq border in the Shiite regions of the country is surely that the Shiites are hostile to their intentions.

Many Arab Sunnis, Arab Shiites, and Kurds, for a variety of reasons, hate the [United Nations] with intensity.

The next few months will tell us whether the Sunnis have decisively separated themselves from the Shiites and Kurds. If they have, we will have no choice but to begin serious counterinsurgency operations throughout the troublesome Arab Sunni zones. Counterinsurgency actions always require lots of low-tech manpower. The American military should have swept through the "Sunni triangle" immediately after the fall of Baghdad, when the ex-Baathists and Sunni fundamentalists were more disorganized than they are now. Hundreds, if not thousands, of ex-Baathists and virulently anti-American Sunni fundamentalists should have been put in detention camps. (Iraq's Kurds and Shiites, about 80 percent of the country's population, would have cheered.) The military brass in Iraq, like many of the State Department civilians first sent to retired Lt. General Jay M. Garner's Office of Reconstruction and Humanitarian Assistance, favored retaining the services of senior Baathists and so failed to move decisively against the remnants of Saddam's regime, believing they were no longer a serious threat. Diehard Baathist military and internal-security officers were allowed to live unharassed. The Pentagon and the State Department must now compensate for past mistakes.

Burden sharing

Rumsfeld and the White House hope to do so, it seems, by introducing more foreign troops. Rumsfeld, a forceful advocate of doing a lot with a small, up-to-date army, probably realizes that counterinsurgency operations may threaten the transformation of his forces. It's difficult to emphasize high-tech, high-impact, and mobility—all worthwhile goals for America's military—when the battlefield at hand demands old-fashioned, labor-intensive, very personal combat. More foreign troops deployed to low-danger police operations in theory would free up American soldiers for conflict in the Sunni triangle. It also might, in theory, allow more U.S. soldiers to go on [leave]. Also, Rumsfeld, who has probably juxtaposed the word "democracy" with "Iraq" less often than any other senior U.S. official, may well see the future of his transformed U.S. military as strategically more important than the future composition of the Iraqi government.

The military brass, like Colin Powell, didn't want to fight this war. They are probably thinking more about an exit strategy for U.S. troops than they are about internal Iraqi politics. Getting more foreign troops in—handing security for Najaf, the seat of the Iraqi Shiite clergy, to the Spaniards—may cause them little anxiety. Ditto for Pakistani, Bangladeshi, or Moroccan troops. For the Pentagon and the White House (unlike the State Department and the Democratic party elite), the use of foreign troops in Iraq is just a pragmatic question. Calling up more National Guard units seems to be out of the question; calling up foreigners isn't.

It's just this type of pragmatism, however, that could irretrievably damage the Bush administration in Iraq and reverse the enormous progress it has made against terrorism. It has been possible—up until now—to find many Pentagon officials who realized, for example, that deploying French or Russian troops to Iraq would probably be highly counterproductive given the pro-Saddam reputation both have among the Shiites. Neither Frenchmen nor Russians are viewed in Iraq or anywhere else in the Middle East as harbingers of democracy.

A despised institution

Neither is the United Nations at all liked in Iraq. Indeed, many Arab Sunnis, Arab Shiites, and Kurds, for a variety of reasons, hate the institution with intensity. Once upon a time, the "right wing" of the Bush administration appeared to be sufficiently attuned to internal Iraqi dynamics to know that having the United Nations on its side was not necessarily beneficial. Many Pentagon and White House officials used to be keenly aware of the need to repair the image of American power in the Muslim Middle East. The war in Iraq was for them never just about finding weapons of mass destruction. Confronting the central tenet of bin Ladenism—that America is weak and cannot hold its ground against true-believers willing to die for the cause—helped animate the administration's fighting spirit after victory in Afghanistan.[2] There is good reason to believe that here, too, the "right wing" of the administration is going wobbly. Negotiating with the French, Germans, and Russians at the United Nations immediately after the bombings in Baghdad and Najaf, as the administration did, clearly sends a signal to all but the blind and deaf that the United States can't take the heat. In the Middle East for the first time since Saddam's fall in April [2003], you can hear the intelligentsia loudly (and hopefully) speculate about the United States' abandoning Iraq.

The sheikhs and the intellectuals may hate us in their hearts; but they absolutely don't want to entrust their property, wives, and daughters to foreign Arab Muslims.

The Bush administration's embrace of odd, counterproductive notions is nowhere more evident than in its energetic pursuit of foreign Muslim troops for Iraq. The reasoning for these deployments—which probably won't happen unless the United States gets the consent of the

---

2. Osama bin Laden's al Qaeda terrorist organization, responsible for the September 11, 2001, terrorist attacks, was based in Afghanistan. Following the September 11 attacks, the United States invaded Afghanistan to uproot al Qaeda and the Taliban government of Afghanistan, which had supported bin Laden.

French, Germans, and Russians at the U.N.—apparently is that Iraqi Muslims would respect foreign Muslim troops more than they respect American soldiers. Leaving aside why in the world the Bush administration would want to deploy Muslim soldiers from nondemocratic countries to Iraq, the Muslim-likes-Muslim sentiment behind this argument is a myth. Middle Eastern history teaches the opposite. Since the dawn of the 19th century Muslim states have shown much greater confidence in the professionalism of Western soldiers than of fellow Muslims. Rulers and intellectuals may say nasty things about Westerners publicly, but privately they have consistently shown that they feel safer with infidels than they do with their own. After the first Gulf War, the Persian Gulf states made a big show of wanting the Egyptians and the Syrians, not the Americans, to assume the responsibility for their security. No Egyptian or Syrian soldier ever landed. The sheikhs and the intellectuals may hate us in their hearts; but they absolutely don't want to entrust their property, wives, and daughters to foreign Arab Muslims.

Iraqi distrust

Shiite Iraqis in particular are acutely conscious that their Arab and Muslim brethren didn't support the war against Saddam. Indeed, Iraqis watched on Arab satellite television with bitter enmity and black humor the antiwar demonstrations throughout the Middle East (and in Europe).

It beggars the imagination to suggest that an Iraqi truck driver on the Amman-Baghdad highway will feel more secure with Moroccans or Bangladeshis doing road checks. It also beggars the imagination to believe that Shiite clerics will feel better knowing that Sunni Pakistanis—who are just a bit below Saudis in the Shiite pantheon of anti-Shiite Sunni fundamentalists—are patrolling their country. And nobody in Iraq is going to feel good about the Turks arriving in force. There is an argument for having the Turks assume certain security tasks in the Arab Sunni belt—Arab Sunnis would probably fear Turkish soldiers far more than they do Americans—but the negatives with the Kurds, who aren't fond of the Turks, and the Shiite clergy, who strongly reject Turkish secularism, easily outweigh the positives with the Arab Sunnis.

None of what the Bush administration is planning to do with foreign soldiers in Iraq makes much sense. Of course, the administration may luck out. The Sunni Arab insurrection in the central lands may blow over without ever testing the mettle and wisdom of the foreign troops spread throughout the country. Maybe no poorly trained, vodka-fond Ukrainian soldier will take liberties with a Shiite lass. Perhaps the foreign soldiers will follow American orders well and interact with the natives in the exemplary way that most American soldiers have done. It's possible. However, if you don't believe in luck in the Middle East, it might be wise to back the French. France's great-gaming and obduracy may just block a U.N. mandate that would unleash more foreign soldiers on Iraqi soil. It would be a delightful irony if Jacques Chirac prevented President Bush from putting the wrong foot forward.

8

The United States Must Increase Its Investment in Rebuilding Iraq

Paul Bremer

Paul Bremer served as the head of the Coalition Provisional Authority, the civilian body established in 2003 by the United States to govern Iraq.

The United States has a clear vision for rebuilding Iraq. The costs to realize this vision will be high in dollars and potentially in lives, but that price must be paid. The $87 billion requested by President George W. Bush for Iraq will work to establish a new justice system, military, and infrastructure, which will bolster the efforts to transform Iraq into a modern and self-sufficient nation. If the United States were to abandon Iraq now, it would fall back into despotism.

Editor's Note: This viewpoint was originally given as testimony before the Senate on September 22, 2003. In it Bremer asks Congress to grant President George W. Bush's request for $87 billion to help rebuild Iraq. Congress granted Bush's request.

B efore I begin, I want to pay tribute to the men and women of our armed services. Leading a coalition, our armed forces delivered a military victory without precedent. In roughly three weeks [in the spring of 2003], they liberated a country larger than Germany and Italy combined. And they did so with forces smaller than the Army of the Potomac.

I know that you and all Americans hate waking up to hear a newscast that begins, "Last night another American solider was killed in Iraq. . . ."

My day starts eight hours ahead of yours. I am among the first to know of those deaths, and no one regrets them more than I do. But these deaths, painful as they are, are not senseless. They are part of the price we pay for civilization, for a world that refuses to tolerate terrorism and genocide and weapons of mass destruction.

Those who ambush coalition forces, . . . are trying to thwart consti-

Paul Bremer, testimony before the U.S. Senate Appropriations Committee, Washington, DC, September 22, 2003.

tutional and democratic government in Iraq. They are trying to create an environment of insecurity. They are in a losing battle with history.

A vision for Iraq

President [George W.] Bush's vision, in contrast, provides for an Iraq made secure through the efforts of Iraqis. In addition to a more secure environment, the President's plan provides for an Iraqi economy based on sound economic principles bolstered by a modern, reliable infrastructure. And finally, the President's plan provides for a democratic and sovereign Iraq at the earliest reasonable date.

Terrorists love state sponsors, countries that provide them with cash, arms, refuge, a protected place to rest and plan future operations. Saddam's Iraq was one of those countries.

If terrorists cannot find a congenial state sponsor, they thrive in chaotic environments with little or no effective government. When militias, warlords, and communities war with each other, terrorists are right at home. Think of Lebanon in the 1980s.

The President's plan provides for a democratic and sovereign Iraq at the earliest reasonable date.

Either outcome, or some combination of both, is possible in Iraq if we do not follow up on our military victory with the wherewithal to win the peace.

The opposite is also true. Creating a sovereign, democratic, constitutional, and prosperous Iraq deals a blow to terrorists. It gives the lie to those who describe us as enemies of Islam, enemies of the Arabs, and enemies of the poor. That is why the President's $87 billion request has to be seen as an important element in the global war on terrorism.[1]

Drawing on history

Our national experience teaches us how to consolidate a military victory.

We did not have that experience 85 years ago when we emerged victorious from World War I. Many had opposed the war, and wished to shake the old world dust off their boots and solve problems at home. We had spent and lent a lot of money. The victors celebrated their victory, mourned their dead, and demanded the money they were owed.

The result was another World War. After that conflict, we showed we had learned that military victory must be followed by a program to secure the peace. In 1948, our greatest generation recognized that military victory was hollow if democracy was not reinforced against tyranny and terrorism.

Democracy could not flourish unless Europe's devastated economies were rebuilt. That generation responded with the boldest, most generous, and most productive act of statesmanship in the past century—the Marshall Plan. Winston Churchill called it "the most unsordid act in history."

---

1. Congress granted President Bush's request.

The Marshall Plan, enacted with overwhelming bipartisan support, set war-torn Europe on the path to the freedom and prosperity that Europeans enjoy today. After a thousand years as a cockpit of war, Europe became a cradle of peace in just two generations.

The need for quick action

The $20.3 billion in grants to Iraq the President seeks as part of this $87 billion supplemental [appropriation] bespeaks grandeur of vision equal to the one which created the free world at the end of World War II. Iraqis living in freedom with dignity will set an example in this troubled region which so often spawns terrorists. A stable, peaceful, economically productive Iraq will serve American interests by making America safer.

No one part of the supplemental is dispensable, and no part is more important than the others. This is a carefully considered request.

This is urgent. The urgency of military operations is self-evident. The funds for nonmilitary action in Iraq are equally urgent. Most Iraqis welcomed us as liberators, and we glowed with the pleasure of that welcome. Now the reality of foreign troops on the streets is starting to chafe. Some Iraqis are beginning to regard us as occupiers and not as liberators. Some of this is inevitable, but faster progress on reconstruction will help.

Unless this supplemental passes quickly, Iraqis face an indefinite period with blackouts eight hours daily. The link to the safety of our troops is indirect, but real. The people who ambush our troops are small in number and do not do so because they have undependable electric supplies. However, the population's view of us is directly linked to their cooperation in hunting down those who attack us. Earlier progress gives us an edge against the terrorists.

We need to emulate the military practice of using overwhelming force in the beginning. Incrementalism and escalation are poor military practice, and they are a poor model for economic assistance.

Iraq has almost $200 billion in debt and reparations hanging over it as a result of Saddam [Hussein's] economic incompetence and aggressive wars. Iraq is in no position to service its existing debt, let alone to take on more. Mountains of unpayable debt contributed heavily to the instability that paved Hitler's path to power. The giants of the post–World War II generation recognized this, and Marshall Plan assistance was overwhelmingly grant aid.

The President's first priority is security—security provided by Iraqis to and for Iraqis. That security extends to our forces and changes Iraq from a logistics and planning base for terrorists into a bulwark against them.

Three pillars of security

The President's supplemental seeks $5.1 billion for three pillars of security.

The first pillar is public safety. If the U.S. Congress agrees to the President's request, we will spend just over $2 billion for police and police training, border enforcement, fire and civil defense, public safety training, and a communications network to link it all together. Already 40,000 police are on duty. Our plan will double this number in the next 18 months.

National defense forces are the second pillar. The President seeks another $2 billion for a new, three-division Iraqi army and a civil defense corps. The first battalion of the New Iraqi Army will graduate on schedule October 4 [2003]. By [summer 2004], Iraq will have 27 battalions trained.

The third pillar is a justice system to rein in the criminal gangs, revenge-seekers, and others who prey on Iraqis every day and make them fear that they will never know the quiet enjoyment that so many of us take for granted.

To fund this justice system, the President requests approximately $1 billion for technical assistance to investigate crimes against humanity, security for witnesses, judges, and prosecutors, and the construction of prisons sufficient to house 16,000 additional inmates.

The benefits of security

This security assistance to Iraq benefits the United States in four ways.

First, Iraqis will be more effective. As talented and courageous as the coalition forces are, they can never replace an Iraqi policeman who knows his beat, who knows his people, their customs, rhythms, and language. Iraqis want Iraqis providing their security, and so do we.

Second, as these Iraqi security forces assume their duties, they replace coalition troops in the roles that generate frustration, friction, and resentment—conducting searches, manning checkpoints, guarding installations.

Third, this frees up coalition forces for the mobile, sophisticated offensive operations against former regime loyalists and terrorists for which they are best suited.

Finally, these new Iraqi forces reduce the overall security demands on coalition forces and speed the day when we can bring troops home.

A stable, peaceful, economically productive Iraq will serve American interests by making America safer.

Security is the first and indispensable element of the President's plan. Security is not, by itself, sufficient to ensure success because a security system resting only on arms is a security system that will fail. Recreating Iraq as a nation at peace with itself and with the world, an Iraq that terrorists will flee rather than flock to, requires more than people with guns.

A good security system cannot persist on the knife edge of economic collapse. When Saddam scurried away from coalition forces, he left behind an economy ruined not by our attacks but by decades of neglect, theft, and mismanagement.

Rebuilding the economy

The Iraqis must refashion their economy. Saddam left them a Soviet-style command economy. That poor model was further hobbled by cronyism, theft, and pharonic self-indulgence by Saddam and his intimates.

Important changes have already begun.

The Iraqi Minister of Finance [in September 2003] announced a set of market-oriented policies that is among the world's boldest. Those policies include a new Central Bank law which grants the Iraqi Central Bank full legal independence, makes price stability the paramount policy objective, and gives the Central Bank full control over monetary and exchange rate policy and broad authority to supervise Iraqi banks. This is rare anywhere in the world and unique in the region.

The Iraqi Government Council proposed and I signed into law a program opening Iraq to foreign investment. Foreign firms may open wholly owned companies or buy 100 percent of Iraqi businesses. Under this law, foreign firms receive national treatment and have an unrestricted right to remit profits and capital.

Iraq's new tax system is admirably straightforward. The highest marginal tax rate on personal and corporate income is 15 percent.

Tariff policy is equally simple. There is a two-year "reconstruction tariff" of 5 percent on all but a few imports.

Foreign banks are free to enter Iraq and will receive equal treatment with Iraqi banks.

On October 15 [2003], Iraq will get a new Dinar, which will float against the world's currencies.[2]

Iraq's pro-growth policies should bring real, sustained growth and protect against something we have all seen and regretted—economic assistance funds disappearing into a morass of poverty.

Protecting economic gains

The Iraqi Government has put in place the legal procedures for encouraging a vibrant private sector. But those policies will come to nothing if Iraq must try to reestablish itself on an insufficient and unreliable electric grid or in a security environment that puts a stick in the spokes of the wheels of commerce.

Iraq cannot realize its potential to return quickly to the world stage as a responsible player without the services essential to a modern society.

We have made significant progress restoring these essential services. The widely predicted humanitarian crisis did not occur. There was no major flow of refugees. All of Iraq's 240 hospitals and 90 percent of its health clinics are open. There is adequate food, and there is no evidence of epidemic. We have cleared thousands of miles of irrigation canals so that farmers in these areas have more water than they have had for a generation. Electrical service will reach pre-war levels within a month.

However, the remaining demands are vast, which is why the President is requesting almost $15 billion for infrastructure programs in Iraq.

Democratizing Iraq

The democratization of Iraq, on which so much global attention is focused, is further advanced than many realize.

Some suggest we should move soon to give full sovereignty to an Iraqi government. I firmly believe that such haste would be a mistake. Iraq has spent a quarter century under a dictatorship as absolute and abusive as that of Nazi Germany. As a result, political distortions and in-

2. The new Iraqi Dinar was introduced as scheduled.

equities permeate the fabric of political life.

No appointed government, even one as honest and dedicated as the Iraqi Governing Council, can have the legitimacy necessary to take on the difficult issues Iraqis face as they write their constitution and elect a government. The only path to full Iraqi sovereignty is through a written constitution, ratified and followed by free, democratic elections.[3]

As you examine the President's plan, I am sure you will see that it is an integrated and thoughtful whole. Every part depends on every other part. As the Congress knows, sweeping political reforms cannot be separated from sweeping economic reforms.

It is equally obvious that a population beleaguered by the threat of terrorism and endless insufficiencies in water, electricity, and telephones finds it hard to concentrate on the virtues of a new constitution and market-oriented economic policies.

The United States must lead in Iraq

The United States must take the lead in restoring Iraq as a friend and democratic model. . . . We must set the example for other nations of goodwill.

When we launched military operations against Iraq, we assumed a great responsibility that extends beyond defeating Saddam's military. We cannot simply pat the Iraqis on the back, tell them they are lucky to be rid of Saddam, and then ask them to go find their place in a global market—to compete without the tools for competition.

To do so would invite economic collapse followed by political extremism and a return to terrorism. If, after coming this far, we turn our backs and let Iraq lapse into factional chaos, some new tyranny, and terrorism, we will have committed a grave error.

Success tells not just Iraqis, but the world that there is hope, that the future is not defined by tyranny on one side and terrorism on the other.

3. An Iraqi interim government assumed full sovereignty on June 28, 2004.

9

America Will Likely Fail to Establish a Democracy in Iraq

Chappell Lawson and Strom C. Thacker

Chappell Lawson is an associate professor of political science at the Massachusetts Institute of Technology. Strom C. Thacker is an associate professor of international relations at Boston University.

An analysis of characteristics common among democratic nations reveals what factors make democracy more likely to succeed. The socioeconomic factors present in Iraq suggest that democracy will not develop in that nation even with the help of the United States. Of the nations invaded or occupied over the last fifty years by the United States, only half have developed lasting democratic institutions. Even if Iraq is unable to achieve full democratization, however, taking steps such as adopting a decentralized form of government, creating proper electoral districts, establishing civilian control of the military, and creating a free press will at least leave Iraq better off than it was under deposed Iraqi dictator Saddam Hussein.

With the fall of Saddam Hussein's regime, politicians, pundits, and scholars have turned their attention toward the task of political reconstruction in Iraq. Can Iraqis, or their American occupiers, build a viable, democratic regime from the rubble of Baathist rule?

So far, the Bush administration has sounded bullish: Secretary of State Colin Powell recently looked forward "to the day when a democratic, representative government at peace with its neighbors leads Iraq to rejoin the family of nations," and President [George W.] Bush personally expressed the belief that democracy could flourish in Iraq in the wake of a U.S. invasion. Even more ambitiously, other administration officials have suggested that regime change in Iraq could trigger reform across the Arab world, with a newly democratic Iraq serving as a model for other countries in the region.

Such arguments about the potential democratization of Iraq have been accompanied by references to the postwar reconstruction of Germany and Japan, which occupation forces effectively remade into liberal-democratic allies of the United States. From this point of view, Iraq is either ready for democracy now or can be made so relatively rapidly under U.S. tutelage. Skeptics have drawn parallels to recent failures of nation-building in Afghanistan, Bosnia-Herzegovina, Haiti, Kosovo, Somalia, and elsewhere. From their perspective, U.S. efforts to promote democracy in Iraq are doomed to failure.

We argue that Iraq is unlikely to sustain democratic institutions, even given protracted U.S. occupation.

Who is right? How realistic is the notion that Iraq will become a democracy after Anglo-American occupation? What sort of impact can the United States expect to have on Iraq's political trajectory? And, whatever the odds, what steps might improve the chances that democracy will survive? We argue that Iraq is unlikely to sustain democratic institutions, even given protracted U.S. occupation. At the same time, we argue that U.S. efforts are not completely hopeless: A series of measures adopted under American occupation would make democracy substantially more likely.

Assessing the odds

In the [spring 2003] issue of [*Hoover Digest*], Larry Diamond wrote:

> It is possible—just possible—that Iraq could gradually develop into a democracy, but the task is huge and the odds are long against it. . . . The social, economic, and political conditions for establishing democracy in Iraq are far from favorable.

We agree; if anything, we find Diamond's view fairly optimistic. Iraq has few of the success factors associated with democracy, such as a high degree of economic development and a Western cultural tradition.

To reach this unfortunate conclusion, we assessed how democratic a country with Iraq's "social, economic, and political conditions" might be expected to be. We first measured levels of democracy in 186 different countries on a numerical scale during 1996–2000, using data compiled by Freedom House [a nonpartisan organization dedicated to fostering freedom]. On this scale, countries such as the United States, Sweden, and Costa Rica scored highest (12 out of a possible 12). At the other end of the spectrum, Iraq under Saddam Hussein scored lowest (zero)—a distinction it shared with countries such as Afghanistan (under the Taliban), Burma, Cuba, Libya, North Korea, Saudi Arabia, Somalia, Sudan, Turkmenistan, and Vietnam. Most nations, of course, fell somewhere in between these extremes; Colombia and Russia, for instance, score close to the middle, indicating that their governments are neither fully democratic nor wholly totalitarian.

For all 186 countries we then gathered measurements of the factors that political scientists have traditionally associated with democracy: literacy; per capita income; socioeconomic inequality; ethnic, linguistic, and religious divisions; past experience with democratic government; history as a British colony; size and geography; whether a country is an energy exporter; whether a country has been involved in a recent war; the percentage of the population that is Muslim; and the region of the world in which a country is located. In general, richer, more literate, more egalitarian, and more homogenous societies do better at establishing and sustaining democratic governance, as do small island states with a history of British or American rule. By contrast, petro-states, countries with mainly Muslim populations, and nations with little cultural affinity for the West all tend to be less democratic.

When we consider all the factors discussed above, we find that a country with Iraq's profile ought to fall somewhere between a zero and a two on the democracy scale. In other words, given what political scientists know about the causes of democracy, Iraq under Saddam Hussein was more or less what one would expect. It thus seems far-fetched to expect that Iraq would become a free society if left to its own devices.

Assessing the U.S. impact

Of course, post-Saddam Iraq will not be left to its own devices; it will be occupied by U.S. and other pro-democratic forces. The next logical question, then, is how occupation might affect Iraq's political prospects. We approach this puzzle in much the same way as we did our analysis of democracy in general: by attempting to measure the impact of U.S. occupation on a country's long-term political development.

By our count, the United States has occupied or helped to occupy 19 countries in the [twentieth] century with the goal of reshaping their political system. These include Afghanistan, Austria, Bosnia-Herzegovina, Cambodia, Cuba, the Dominican Republic, Germany, Grenada, Haiti, Japan, the Marshall Islands, Micronesia, Nicaragua, Palau, Panama, the Philippines, Somalia, South Korea, and South Vietnam. Democratization was not always the most important goal behind these occupations, but in all of these cases, U.S. forces attempted to leave behind something resembling a set of democratic institutions. In about half of these cases, democratic institutions lasted; in the others, they did not.

Given what political scientists know about the causes of democracy, Iraq under Saddam Hussein was more or less what one would expect.

The scope and duration of occupation differed substantially, so it is not an easy matter to assess how transformative or thorough the experience of U.S. rule actually was. One simplistic way to do so is to divide the 19 cases into two groups: (1) those where intervention was truncated or incomplete and (2) those where the United States stayed for a reasonably long period of time and made a concerted attempt to restructure the country's political and social systems. Bosnia-Herzegovina, Cambodia,

Grenada, Somalia, and South Korea fall into the first group. By contrast, Austria, Cuba, the Dominican Republic, Germany, Haiti, Japan, the Marshall Islands, Micronesia, Nicaragua, Palau, Panama, the Philippines, and South Vietnam clearly experienced more thoroughgoing and protracted occupation. Because our measures of democracy pre-date the U.S. invasion of Afghanistan, and because it is too soon to tell what will come from the allied occupation, we exclude that case from our discussion.

Even if American efforts fall short of full democratization, the United States may be able to leave Iraqis substantially better off than they were before the invasion.

Contrary to what might be expected, the impact of the United States is not particularly impressive. On average, countries in the second category score only about one and a half points higher on the democracy scale than countries that were never occupied. Countries that were occupied briefly actually score a couple of points lower.

When we take into account the other factors discussed above, such as a country's level of economic development and its cultural affinity with the West, even the impact of protracted occupation fades into insignificance. In other words, the countries that became democratic after U.S. occupation were already much more likely to become so; the countries that failed to become democratic were always unlikely to make the transition. At best, U.S. occupation seems to exercise only a modest and indirect influence on a country's long-term political development. There is, alas, little evidence on which to base a hope that the Anglo-American occupation will dramatically change the prospects for democracy in Iraq.

Taking the right steps

Of course, long odds against democracy should not be an excuse to give up on Iraq altogether. Even if Iraq is unlikely to sustain fully democratic institutions, the degree to which future governments are more or less repressive could vary tremendously. The degree of political openness found in Jordan or Kuwait, for instance, is well worth striving for, even though neither country is a democracy. Even if American efforts fall short of full democratization, the United States may be able to leave Iraqis substantially better off than they were before the invasion.

There is another reason not to give up: We know vastly more today than we did several decades ago about what makes democracy succeed. If these lessons are kept in mind, U.S. efforts to establish democracy may thus prove much more effective than they did in, say, Nicaragua during the 1920s or South Vietnam during the 1960s. In particular, Americans would do well to consider the following steps:

Avoid the curse of oil. One of the biggest dangers facing postwar Iraq is the prospect of its becoming a classic petro-state (such as Nigeria, Libya, or Venezuela), in which vast revenues from the sale of oil accrue to a politically shaky and unrepresentative national government. To avoid such problems, Iraq should adopt some version of the Alaska model, in which each citizen would receive a direct payment from oil revenues. The effects of this system would be to put the country's wealth directly into the hands of Iraqis, to remove discretionary authority from the national government, and to establish the relationship between taxation and spending that characterizes normal states.

Choose parliamentarism over presidentialism. In developing countries, presidential systems tend to concentrate too much power in the hands of one individual, who may then be tempted to ride roughshod over other political actors. Consequently, European-style parliamentary systems are more likely to survive than those that rely on a directly elected chief executive. America encouraged the defeated Axis powers to adopt parliamentary systems; it should do the same in Iraq today.

Adopt a federal system. Although unitary (non-federal) systems may offer certain advantages in administrative efficiency and policy efficacy, in countries with deep, geographically based divisions, some degree of federalism can help democracy succeed. For this reason, Iraq should follow the example of many other democratizing countries by investing state and local governments with real power. Kurds in the north, Sunni Arabs in the center, and Shia Arabs in the south could all be given substantial autonomy within their domains; for the Kurds, in particular, such an arrangement is probably crucial to preventing irredentist rebellion. The process of forming local governments can start now, before any national system is fully constituted.

> *The specter of military rule looms large in a country like Iraq, with a long history of coups and attempted coups.*

Create an electoral branch of government. In any political transition, the first few electoral contests are crucial to democratic success. These founding elections teach political actors to channel their energies into vote-getting, rather than into more polarizing or destructive styles of participation. The initial role of conducting and overseeing elections should rightly fall to foreigners, but eventually the task must be turned over to Iraqis. To this end, Iraq will need a virtual fourth branch of government charged with administering elections. The heads of this supreme electoral authority should be chosen by a two-thirds vote in the congress and given enough funding from domestic or foreign sources to ensure their technical capacity.

Draw electoral districts the right way. The way electoral districts are drawn can play an important role in moderating ethnic divisions and in shaping the way that political parties develop. Perhaps the best approach would be to divide Iraq into a relatively small number of large districts, whose boundaries matched those of Iraq's three major ethnic groupings (Kurd, Sunni Arab, and Shia Arab). Such a system would promote cross-cutting cleavages and help prevent the emergence of any permanent majority. For instance, a party that purported to represent Shia Arabs might do well in districts drawn across major ethnic lines because Shia Arabs in the district might pool their votes to support it against a non-Shia opponent. But in our system, all voters and candidates in a given district would be Shia Arab, so electoral mobilization based on Shia identity would make little sense. At the same time, any political figure who thought that she could win just a small percentage of the vote would have a strong incentive to set up a new party that could siphon votes away from the main Shia party. Electoral politics would thus come to reflect a range of identities—religious, linguistic, class, clan, policy oriented, and so forth—rather than any one polarized division.

Ensure civilian control of the military. Most democracies that collapse do so because government officials with guns (i.e., the security forces) seize power from government officials without guns (i.e., civilian politicians). The specter of military rule looms large in a country like Iraq, with a long history of coups and attempted coups. Although there is no single formula for doing so, the experiences of countries such as Argentina, Brazil, and South Korea suggest the following steps: (a) limit the size of the military overall, especially the army; (b) purge the officer corps of those responsible for gross violations of human rights and integrate Shia and Kurdish troops; (c) civilianize any intelligence services, military-run companies, and the defense department; and (d) explicitly confine the military's official mission to external defense, leaving internal security and law enforcement to civilian police.

Build a free press. In most developing countries, mass media are controlled by politicized state monopolies (Eastern Europe, Africa, and Asia) or private oligarchs who trade favorable coverage for political influence (Latin America). Such a sad state of affairs can be avoided by placing state-owned media under the direction of professionalized, politically insulated boards, whose own appointments require supermajorities in the legislature, and by creating a system for allocating private broadcasting concessions that is likewise insulated from direct executive control. In addition, a variety of legal protections for the press—including laws on freedom of information and the protection of the confidentiality of journalistic sources—can help create mass media capable of fulfilling their watchdog role.

In the end, it is unlikely that Iraq will become a full-fledged democracy on the American or European mold in the near future. That said, certain institutions may well survive once occupation forces leave the country. Even if Iraq becomes a semi-authoritarian state, Iraqis will remain substantially better off than they were under Saddam Hussein's brutal regime. Drawing on the experiences of the last several decades can help ensure that outcome.

10

U.S. Troops Are Aiding Rebuilding Efforts in Iraq

Max Boot

Max Boot is a senior fellow at the Council on Foreign Relations, a non-partisan think tank. He was the editorial features editor for the Wall Street Journal, *and has contributed articles to the* New York Times, Christian Science Monitor, *and other publications.*

U.S. soldiers are succeeding in Iraq. Their complex mission requires them to suppress Iraqi insurgents and aid the general population. Their efforts have been recognized by Iraqis, particularly in the southern portion of Iraq, where U.S. soldiers are generally supported and welcomed by the Iraqi people. The military still faces challenges, however, particularly in dealing with the ineffective Coalition Provisional Authority, the U.S.-run civilian government in Iraq. [As this volume went to press, the Coalition Provisional Authority had been dissolved.]

I went to Iraq in August [2003], the day after a bomb had ripped through the United Nations compound in Baghdad, killing 23 people including the U.N. special envoy. I came home the day after another massive car bomb exploded at a mosque in Najaf, taking more than 95 lives including that of a leading cleric. Yet I returned more optimistic than when I went.

Understandably, these attacks have caused apprehension, verging on panic, among U.S.-based commentators and politicians. A chorus of critics is already attacking the Bush administration for losing Iraq. During my trip I, too, saw plenty of room for improvement, especially by the civilian-run Coalition Provisional Authority [CPA] in Baghdad. For that matter, I was almost a casualty of a roadside bomb myself. Nevertheless, after 10 days traveling with soldiers and Marines in both the north and south, I am encouraged by the resourcefulness of our troops and struck by how different things look when seen firsthand. From afar, chaos seems to reign in Iraq; up close, distinct signs of progress emerge.

Air travel isn't one of the more positive signs. There still is no commercial air service to Iraq. I went in with Bing West, a former assistant secretary of defense and a Marine veteran of Vietnam, on a Marine Lear jet from Kuwait to Al Kut in central Iraq. From there, an old CH-46 helicopter whisked us to the 1st Marine Division headquarters at Camp Babylon. Yes, that Babylon. The former home of Nebuchadnezzar now houses rulers clad in khaki camouflage.

Life at Camp Babylon

The headquarters of the 1st Marine Division was on the grounds of one of [former Iraqi leader] Saddam Hussein's numerous palaces. A guest house had been turned into a Combat Operations Center where officers and enlisted personnel sat at laptop computers monitoring everything from enemy attacks to electricity flows. A tent city around the building was full to overflowing when we arrived. The Marines were in the process of transitioning out, while Poles, Romanians, Bulgarians, Hungarians, Spaniards, and numerous other coalition troops had already arrived to take their place. The formal handoff to the coalition forces occurred on September 3 [2003], except in Najaf, where the recent bombing has delayed it.

For Marines who went through the war sleeping in the dirt and eating MREs (Meals Ready to Eat), life at Camp Babylon had gotten relatively civilized by the end of their tour. Most of the tents had cots and air conditioning, "head" calls could be taken in the privacy of a port-o-potty, and food came from a "chow hall" run by Indian contract employees. Things will be positively luxurious for the allied troops, who are having built for them, at U.S. expense, air-conditioned shower and laundry facilities. The food wasn't bad—we had lobster my first night and excellent cakes—but everyone from buck private to three-star general waited in a long line before getting fed.

From here the 1st Marine Division directed battalions that ran all of south-central Iraq—up to 11 million people in the Shiite heartland. Major General James Mattis laughingly called it the Blue Diamond Republic of Iraq, after the 1st Division's nickname. If so, he was president of the republic, or, more accurately, its benevolent dictator. Mattis is a legend inside the Marine Corps, having led the Marines into both Afghanistan and Iraq. He was so hell-bent on reaching Baghdad that he fired one of his brigade commanders for not going fast enough. It was his men who toppled the statue of Saddam Hussein in central Baghdad on April 9 [2003], signaling the end of the war.

The general in charge

Relatively short and trim, with a silver crewcut and owlish spectacles, Mattis doesn't look particularly imposing. But when he opens his mouth it becomes apparent that he's cut from the George S. Patton mold. Funny, blunt, erudite, inspiring, and profane, he takes no guff and tolerates no inefficiency. At nightly briefings with his staff, he dissected PowerPoint presentations with laser-like questions that got to the heart of every problem. The issues he dealt with were more appropriate to an imperial proconsul than to a general: how to combat Islamic extremists, win over ordinary people, distribute fuel, enforce law and order, and a thousand other matters. Mattis was not the least bit fazed by the challenge.

And he had made substantial progress. While Baghdad and the Sunni Triangle [where Sunni Arabs are concentrated] were still plagued by anti-American terrorism, life in the Blue Diamond Republic was pretty calm. It might not seem that way in the wake of the August 29 [2003] car bombing in Najaf. But despite that event, a substantial degree of normality had returned to Najaf and neighboring towns. The streets I saw were bustling, and the Marines enjoyed excellent relations with local leaders.

Not the least of their achievement is that no Marine has been killed by hostile fire since May 1 [2003], when President [George W.] Bush proclaimed "major hostilities" at an end. Almost 70 Army soldiers have been slain in that period.[1] This success isn't a result of flooding south-central Iraq with soldiers. Mattis never deployed more than 8,000 Marines, along with some Army civil affairs, psychological operations, and military police units, to control an area the size of Missouri.

The issues [Mattis] dealt with [included] how to combat Islamic extremists, win over ordinary people, distribute fuel, enforce law and order, and a thousand other matters. Mattis was not the least bit fazed by the challenge.

There is no doubt that the Marines' task was made easier by the fact that the Shiites suffered under the old regime and welcomed their liberation. But few analysts predicted in May [2003] that Shiite holy cities like Najaf and Karbala would emerge as strongholds of pro-American sentiment. Much of the talk back then was of Iranian infiltration and Lebanese-style terrorism. That hasn't happened, at least not against Americans, and every single Marine I met was convinced that the reason had to do with their approach to peacekeeping, which they believe superior to the more heavy-handed methods employed, at least initially, by Army units that occupied Baghdad and the Sunni area to the immediate north and west.

Three guiding principles

The Marine strategy was based on three principles. First, do no harm. That meant not alienating Iraqis by violating their religious or social customs. Women, for instance, should not be subject to intrusive searches. When talking to Iraqis, Marines were instructed to point their firearms away and take off their sunglasses. Above all, it meant using as little firepower as possible. As Mattis put it: "If someone needs shooting, shoot him. If someone doesn't need shooting, protect him."

The Marines showed restraint when dealing with hostile crowds. They did not have a single incident like the one that occurred in Fallujah in late April [2003], when the 82nd Airborne opened fire on a crowd of demonstrators, killing at least 12. Marines were more likely to greet hos-

---

1. As this volume went to press, more than 1000 U.S. troops had died in Iraq.

tile crowds with free bottles of water than with bullets, on the assumption that someone can't be too angry with you if he's just accepted some water from you.

The Marines' second guiding principle was to win hearts and minds. The Marines repaired schools, distributed candy, handed out free medical supplies, set up Rotary clubs, and undertook myriad other charitable tasks. This earned them goodwill among the community leading to increased intelligence about troublemakers.

Their third principle was to be ready to win a 10-second gunfight. While wanting to be as open and friendly as possible, all Marines were told to be ready to open fire at a moment's notice. When Army supply convoys get attacked by fedayeen, they speed away, I was told. When Marine convoys got hit, they were supposed to stop immediately and disgorge infantrymen to pursue the attackers, Mattis insisted that even convoys carrying the Marines out of Iraq retain a robust offensive capability.

It all adds up to Mattis's widely publicized slogan: "No Better Friend, No Worse Enemy" than a U.S. Marine. To see how this yin-yang policy was carried out, we toured some Marine units just before they headed home.

Task Force Scorpion

Our first stop was in the desert southwest of Baghdad, home to a giant Army logistics base called Dogwood. This area is different from the rest of the Blue Diamond Republic because it's primarily Sunni, not Shiite, and it's experienced some of the same security woes that have plagued the Sunni Triangle. In May and June [2003], Army convoys operating here suffered nonstop guerrilla attacks. During one two-week period in May [2003] there were 51 ambushes.

Although this was an Army base, it was in the Marines' area of operations, so Mattis set up Task Force Scorpion to clean up the mess. Composed of the 4th Force Reconnaissance (the closest the egalitarian Marines come to having Special Forces), the 4th Light Armored Regiment, some Army civil affairs soldiers, and a couple of Marine infantry platoons, the task force never totaled more than 1,000 soldiers.

As Mattis put it: "If someone needs shooting, shoot him. If someone doesn't need shooting, protect him."

But with aggressive patrolling, it managed to capture a number of terrorists and reduce the number of attacks. Just before we arrived they had nabbed a Republican Guard general and a four-man team that had been mortaring Dogwood. The successful operations impressed the local people, who flooded them with unsolicited tips. Based on that information they staged surgical raids that usually involved no gunfire and resulted in the surrender of a suspect. While aggressive against suspected terrorists, the task force's commanding officer, Lieutenant Colonel Andrew Pappas, regularly met with local sheikhs.

As we were being briefed on Scorpion's operations, an officer volunteered that they were planning a raid that very night. Would we like to go along? Sure, I said, little suspecting what I was getting myself into.

Reveille came in total darkness at 4:30 A.M. on Friday, August 22 [2003], though the crump of a mortar shell landing several hundred meters from our barracks already had me wide awake. By 5:30 [A.M.] we were on the move. Our target was a suspected Baathist leader who had escaped a previous raid by jumping into the Euphrates and swimming away in his underwear. We were headed once again to his posh riverside home about an hour and a half from Dogwood.

The successful operations impressed the local people, who flooded [the Marines] with unsolicited tips.

Force Recon Marines, riding in two Humvees, were supposed to conduct the raid. Three light armored vehicles went along to "sanitize" the perimeter and deal with any "squirters," or fleeing suspects. Dressed in a heavy flak vest and Kevlar helmet, I was squished into the back of one of these tinpots. Without enough room to sit up straight or stretch out my legs, and with virtually no portholes, I was left to stare for hours on end at pictures of a soldier's girlfriend and a pinup of Pamela Anderson, both attached by magnets to the vehicle hull. Soon the temperature would soar over 120 degrees. Dust wafted through two open hatches manned by Marines with M-16s.

Unexpected action

At about 6 A.M., our journey took an unexpected twist. As we were driving by some fields, three remote-controlled bombs exploded by the side of the road. Each was made from a 155 mm shell packed with explosives. Two more unexploded bombs were later discovered by the roadside, one of them full of white phosphorus. Had they all gone off when intended, hundreds of pounds of explosives would have ripped into our column, almost certainly causing serious casualties. Luckily the mission commander, Major Joe Cabell, insisted on proper dispersion and the explosions passed harmlessly between our vehicles.

As soon as the attack occurred, the column pulled over to the side of the road and Marines jumped out to hunt for the perpetrators. A gunner saw what he thought were men fleeing through the fields and fired warning shots. It's a good thing he didn't hit anyone: It later turned out they were innocent farmers. As two Huey helicopters buzzed some nearby palm trees, it started to look like a scene from a Vietnam War movie.

With the help of an interpreter, the Marines interviewed local farmers and found out that a suspicious blue van had been seen in the neighborhood. We set off to find it and eventually ran down a blue Volkswagen van. Its sole occupant, a defiant young man in a track suit, tested positive for gunpowder residue on his hands. The Marines handcuffed him with plexicuffs and tossed him into the back of the light armored vehicle right next to your correspondent. The corporal asked me to "cover" the suspect. I held the 9 mm pistol a bit nervously (I'm more comfortable in think tanks than battle tanks) but did as I was told. In a few minutes, the suspect, his head covered in a T-shirt, was transferred to a Humvee for transportation back to base.

We pressed on with the raid, but it turned out the target wasn't home. We tried a couple of nearby locations—no dice. By 1:30 P.M. we were back at base, hot, filthy, and exhausted. What was supposed to be a four-hour raid had turned into an eight-hour trek across the countryside. I was whipped, but the Marines weren't too discouraged. "It was a good day," said Corporal Daiman Benney, a 26-year-old infantryman with a blond mustache. Reflecting on his impending departure for home, he sighed, "I'll miss chasing bad guys."

Soccer balls and democracy

This is the sharp end of the Marine occupation. The next day we saw the warriors' soft side during a visit to Karbala, site of the second-holiest Shiite shrine. Lieutenant Colonel Matthew Lopez, commander of the 3rd Battalion, 7th Marine Regiment, was preparing to turn over command to a Bulgarian contingent, but before he did so, he had some errands to run. He piled into an SUV accompanied by a sergeant and Bing and me. None of us was wearing a flak vest or helmet. The Marines were in their "soft covers," aka cloth hats. Crammed into the back were dozens of silver soccer balls donated by Nike. The Marines were planning to hand out 15,000 balls to the children of Iraq, and Lopez wanted to make a start today.

As we crawled through the crowded city streets, we tossed soccer balls to any kids we saw.

As we crawled through the crowded city streets, we tossed soccer balls to any kids we saw. As soon as the first ball came bouncing out, a tremendous excitement seized the urchins. They ran after the SUV, arms outstretched, shouting "Mistah! Mistah!" The kids were ecstatic and so was Lopez. With a big smile on his face, he said, "I wish I could take all of them home with me."

When the ball supply was exhausted, we headed to city hall for Lopez's last meeting with the provincial governor and city council. They were as happy to see him as the kids. A consummate diplomat, Lopez exchanged flowery courtesies with a long line of sheikhs and other local officials, and then got down to business. Speaking through his interpreter (a Marine private born in Kuwait), he spent 45 minutes wheeling and dealing over a variety of public works projects. A Bulgarian colonel who will soon replace Lopez looked on to learn how it's done. "You will be missed a lot," a local worthy told Lopez, but the Marine is confident that the people of Karbala are well on the way to self-government. "Democracy is embedded here," he said.

That may be a stretch, but there is no question that the U.S. occupation has made tremendous strides among the Shiites, who comprise 60 percent of Iraq's population. Driving through towns like Karbala and Najaf you see shops overflowing with goods and Iraqi cops in blue uniforms

directing traffic. Violence hasn't entirely disappeared, as witness the August 29 car-bomb murder of Ayatollah Hakim and scores of his followers,
but little animosity is directed toward the Americans, who are generally
seen as liberators.

Every drive through Iraq in a U.S. military vehicle becomes a referen-
dum on the occupation. Do the people smile or frown as you pass? In the
Sunni Triangle, U.S. Army patrols are often met with sullen stares. In central Iraq, smiles and thumbs up are commonplace. Little kids are especially enthusiastic. I felt like the queen of England waving regally at Iraqis
as we drove by in our three-Humvee convoy.

Shiite opposition

Support for the occupation isn't universal, of course. There are still some
clerics who want a theocracy, and they have received support from Iran
and other sources. But they have gained little traction among Iraqis. The
most prominent troublemaker, Moqtada al-Sadr, scion of a family of
prominent ayatollahs, appears to be rapidly losing support, as judged by
the sparse attendance at his sermons in Najaf. The attack on Ayatollah
Hakim was the extremists' attempt to win through violence what they
could not achieve by peaceful means—an attempt that will almost surely
backfire by uniting the Shiites against the barbarians who desecrated their
holiest shrine.

There was pressure from some U.S. officials in the Coalition Provisional Authority to arrest Sadr because of widespread rumors that he was
involved in the murder of a pro-American imam back in April [2003]. But
in the absence of hard evidence, the Marines refused to move against
him. In their view, arresting him would only have turned him into a mar-
tyr. Better to let his rival clerics steal away his support—which seems to
be happening.

CPA: "Can't Provide Anything"

This is only one example of the rifts that divide the military from the
CPA, led by Ambassador L. Paul Bremer.[2] It was apparent during our visit
that the CPA has done little to help the men and women in uniform;
some joked that the agency's initials stand for "Can't Provide Anything."
Even well-intentioned CPA initiatives have been badly bungled.

For instance, there was a plan to put 300,000 unemployed Iraqis to
work clearing agricultural canals. A good idea, but the Iraqi managers
failed to pay the workers for three weeks. In Diwaniyah, a major town in
central Iraq, the unhappy ditch diggers rioted in protest and destroyed a
government building. The Marines, who had not been involved in setting
up this program, were called in to deal with the resulting chaos. They dis-
persed the rioters and paid the agricultural workers out of their own
funds. Now they have set up a system to ensure that the payments are
made. One can only hope that the coalition forces who are replacing the
Marines will prove equally adept at covering for the CPA's missteps.

2. The CPA was dissolved on June 28, 2004, when the Iraqi interim government assumed sovereignty.

Much of the problem, no doubt, is that the CPA lacks the readymade infrastructure available to a military division. Starting from scratch, it has a hard time recruiting qualified candidates to come to Iraq. And those it hires are likely to leave after a few months. Former New York City police chief Bernard Kerik, for instance, arrived at the beginning of the summer to run the justice ministry, and he's already going home. But despite having a small organization, Bremer appears to be centralizing many operations in Baghdad. This is an odd choice given the vast differences between the Kurdish and Arab north, Sunni center, and Shiite south. Running everything from the capital seems a big mistake.

With the 101st Airborne

Complaints about over-centralization are echoed by the 101st Airborne Division. Like the Marines, the "Screaming Eagles" fought in the war, then were called upon to garrison a large chunk of the country—the north—that is moving toward peace and prosperity. The division is headquartered in Mosul, Iraq's second largest city, with a population of 1.2 million. The 101st's entire area of operations encompasses 6 million people, including Arabs, Kurds, Turkomen, and other ethnic groups.

Like the Marines, the 101st is living in one of Saddam's palaces. Its accommodations are slightly more posh; the troops have access to running water, the Internet, satellite TV, even two swimming pools. But only a sadist would begrudge them a few creature comforts. The Marines are heading home in September [2003], the 101st will be here until February 2004, a whole year. One of its brigades, the 3rd, came here after spending most of 2002 in Afghanistan; now the "Rakkasans," as they're called, are deployed in the wasteland between Mosul and the Syrian border.

I felt like the queen of England waving regally at Iraqis as we drove by in our three-Humvee convoy.

The 101st faces many thorny problems unique to its area, such as land disputes between Arabs and Kurds, and a porous border with Syria. But its approach is similar to that of the Marines. In their combat operations center, the division commander, Major General David Petraeus, has posted a sign that proclaims, "We are in a race to win over the people. What have you and your element done to contribute to that goal today?"

They have done a good deal—almost all of it without the help of the CPA. On his own initiative, General Petraeus decided to open the Syrian border to increase trade, and to strike deals with Turkey and Syria to swap Iraqi oil for badly needed electricity. The division has also restored telephone service and is taking bids for cellular service.

Like Mattis, Petraeus preaches respect for Iraqis. Politeness and restraint are the order of the day. And when his troops do have to use strongarm tactics, they take pains not to leave hurt feelings behind. After they killed Uday and Qusay Hussein on July 22 [2003], the division spent more than $100,000 to repair damage to the neighborhood where the intense firefight occurred.

Rebuilding the north

One of the 101st's brigade commanders, Colonel Joe Anderson, hopped in a Humvee to take Bing West and me on a whirlwind tour of Mosul. Projects underway range from training the Iraqi police to providing medicine for a local hospital to painting schools to refurbishing an Olympic-size swimming pool to building houses for refugees. The list seems endless—and the 101st is doing all of it with its commanders' own discretionary fund, much of which comes from seized assets of the old regime.

Aside from providing money for the military to spend, Bremer's Coalition Provisional Authority has as little presence in the north as it has in the south. Its TV station, the Iraqi Media Network, is not received here, thus ceding the propaganda war to anti-American outlets like Al Jazeera. And it has failed to remedy the electricity and fuel problems that plague the entire country. The northern region has less power now than it did a few weeks ago because the central government in Baghdad is siphoning its power to the center, much as Saddam used to.

It was apparent during our visit that the CPA has done little to help the men and women in uniform; some joked that the agency's initials stand for "Can't Provide Anything."

After visiting both northern and southern Iraq, one gets the clear sense that the CPA needs to take a different tack. The same might be said of the Army units that garrison Baghdad and the Sunni areas to the immediate north and west—the 4th Infantry Division, 1st Armored Division, and 3rd Armored Cavalry Regiment. All are armor units less attuned to the demands of peacekeeping than light infantry outfits like the 1st Marine Division and the 101st Airborne. One officer of the 101st suggested that the situation in Baghdad would be much better if his division, with its more nuanced approach, had garrisoned the capital. The Marines, too, are convinced they could do a better job there, which makes it all the more unfortunate that they are now heading home.

In the view of numerous 101st Airborne and 1st Marine officers I talked to, sending more troops to Iraq isn't the answer. Smarter policing tactics and better intelligence are what's required, and training more Iraqi cops should be the top priority. They could use more funding for such training and other reconstruction projects, since, as Petraeus says, "money is ammunition."

Hope for the future

In spite of continuing attacks and various other frustrations, both the 101st Division and the 1st Marine Division display a fundamental optimism about Iraq and its future. As General Petraeus put it, "I think we're winning up here. We have very good momentum." General Mattis delivered the message in an earthier style: "We've got the bastards on the run."

Yet the world press, which lavished such attention on Iraqi looting back in May [2003], seems largely indifferent to the successful work of re-building that has gone on since. The media naturally focus on bombings and shootings, not on the reopening of schools or training of police offi-cers. There is a real danger of another Tet Offensive—an American mili-tary victory turned into a public relations disaster back home.

As we flew back to Kuwait on a UH-60 Blackhawk helicopter, my thoughts were not on such cosmic strategic questions. Rather, I thought of the American men and women who are serving in Iraq. They have per-formed their work with incredible fortitude, humanity, ingenuity, and skill under difficult and often dangerous circumstances. For me, visiting Iraq was a 10-day adventure; for them, it is a 24/7 occupation.

I asked my Marine driver, a wispy-thin 22-year-old lance corporal named William Eberly, why he'd enlisted. "I wanted to feel like I actually did something for my country," he told me, "so I could call myself a true American." It strikes me that Lance Corporal Eberly has done a lot for two countries—the United States and Iraq—whether his countrymen appreci-ate it or not.

Organizations to Contact

The editors have compiled the following list of organizations concerned with the issues debated in this book. The descriptions are derived from materials provided by the organizations. All have publications or information available for interested readers. The list was compiled on the date of publication of the present volume; the information provided here may change. Be aware that many organizations take several weeks or longer to respond to inquiries, so allow as much time as possible.

American Enterprise Institute (AEI)
1150 Seventeenth St. NW, Washington, DC 20036
(202) 862-580 • fax: (202) 862-7177
Web site: www.aei.org

The American Enterprise Institute for Public Policy Research is a scholarly research institute that is dedicated to preserving limited government, private enterprise, and a strong foreign policy and national defense. Its publications on Iraq include articles in its magazine *American Enterprise* and books including *Study of Revenge: The First World Trade Center Attack and Saddam Hussein's War Against America*. Articles, speeches, and seminar transcripts on Iraq are available on its Web site.

The Brookings Institution
1775 Massachusetts Ave. NW, Washington, DC 20036
(202) 797-6000 • fax: (202) 797-6004
e-mail: brookinfo@brook.edu • Web site: www.brookings.org

The institution, founded in 1927, is a think tank that conducts research and education in foreign policy, economics, government, and the social sciences. Its Saban Center for Middle East Policy develops programs to promote a better understanding of policy choices in the Middle East. Articles on Iraq can be found on the organization's Web site and in its publication, including the quarterly *Brookings Review*.

The Carnegie Endowment for International Peace
1779 Massachusetts Ave. NW, Washington, DC 20036
(202) 483-7600
e-mail: info@ceip.org • Web site: www.ceip.org

The Carnegie Endowment is a nonpartisan, nonprofit organization seeking to increase cooperation and understanding between nations, and encourage active international involvement by the United States. In addition to the reports and analysis available on its Web site, the Carnegie Endowment publishes the monthly *Foreign Policy* magazine.

Center for Strategic and International Studies (CSIS)
1800 K St. NW, Suite 400, Washington, DC 20006
(202) 887-0200 • fax: (202) 775-3199
Web site: www.csis.org

The center works to provide world leaders with strategic insights and policy options on current and emerging global issues. It publishes books, including *The "Instant" Lessons of the Iraq War*, the *Washington Quarterly*, a journal on political, economic, and security issues, and other publications, including reports that can be downloaded from its Web site.

Council on Foreign Relations
58 E. Sixty-eighth St., New York, NY 10021
(212) 434-9400 • fax: (212) 434-9800
e-mail: communications@cfr.org • Web site: www.cfr.org

The Council on Foreign Relations is a nonpartisan organization dedicated to the study and sharing of ideas related to the foreign policy of the United States. Articles on Iraq, the war on terror, and a host of other topics can be found on its Web site and in its bimonthly magazine *Foreign Affairs*.

Education for Peace in Iraq Center (EPIC)
1101 Pennsylvania Ave. SE, Washington, DC 20003
(202) 543-6176
e-mail: info@epic-usa.org • Web site: http://epic-usa.org

The organization works to improve humanitarian conditions in Iraq and protect the human rights of Iraq's people. It opposed both international economic sanctions and U.S. military action against Iraq. Articles on Iraq are available on its Web site.

Hoover Institution
Stanford University, Stanford, CA 94305-6010
(650) 723-1754 • fax: (650) 723-1687
Web site: www-hoover.stanford.edu

The Hoover Institution is a public policy research center devoted to advanced study of politics, economics, and political economy—both domestic and foreign—as well as international affairs. It publishes the quarterly *Hoover Digest*, which often includes articles on Iraq, the Middle East, and the war on terrorism, as well as a newsletter and special reports.

International Crisis Group
1629 K St. NW, Suite 450, Washington, DC 20006
(202) 785-1601 • fax: (202) 785-1630
Web site: www.crisisweb.org

The International Crisis Group is a multinational nonprofit organization that is dedicated to finding peaceful, diplomatic solutions to violent conflicts around the world. It regularly publishes analysis and suggestions for world leaders on its Web site. A series of articles on Iraq can be found there.

The Iraq Foundation
1012 Fourteenth St. NW, Suite 1110, Washington, DC 20005
(202) 347-4662 • fax: (202) 347-7897
e-mail: iraq@iraqfoundation.org • Web site: www.iraqfoundation.org

The Iraq Foundation is a nonprofit, nongovernmental organization working for democracy and human rights in Iraq, and for a better international understanding of Iraq's potential as a contributor to political stability and economic progress in the Middle East. Information on its projects as well as other information on Iraq can be found on its Web site.

Middle East Forum
1500 Walnut St., Suite 1050, Philadelphia, PA 19102
(215) 546-5406 • fax: (215) 546-5409
e-mail: info@meforum.org • Web site: www.meforum.org

The Middle East Forum is a think tank that works to define and promote American interests in Iraq and other parts of the Middle East. It supports strong American ties with Israel, Turkey, and other democracies as they emerge. It publishes the *Middle East Quarterly*, a policy-oriented journal. Its Web site includes articles on Iraq and other topics as well as a discussion forum.

Middle East Policy Council
1730 M St. NW, Suite 512, Washington, DC 20036-4505
(202) 296-6767 • fax: (202) 296-5791
e-mail: info@mepc.org • Web site: www.mepc.org

The Middle East Policy Council was founded in 1981 to expand public discussion and understanding of issues affecting U.S. policy in the Middle East. The council is a nonprofit educational organization that operates nationwide. Articles on Iraq can be found in the *Middle East Policy Journal*, its quarterly publication, and on its its Web site.

Middle East Research and Information Project (MERIP)
1500 Massachusetts Ave. NW, Washington, DC 20005
(202) 223-3677 • fax: (202) 223-3604
Web site: www.merip.org

MERIP is a nonprofit, nongovernmental organization with no links to any religious, educational, or political organizations in the United States or elsewhere. Its mission is to educate the public about the contemporary Middle East with particular emphasis on U.S. foreign policy, human rights, and social justice issues. It publishes the bimonthly *Middle East Report*.

Project for the New American Century
1150 Seventeenth St. NW, Washington, DC 20036
(202) 293-4983
Web site: www.newamericancentury.org

The Project for the New American Century is a conservative think tank advocating an increased role for American leadership in the global arena. The project proposes that the United States, through a combination of military strength, diplomacy, and a commitment to moral principle can improve the global situation. Its Web site contains policy briefs, position papers, and editorials on issues related to national defense and global security.

U.S. Department of State, Bureau of Near Eastern Affairs
2201 C St. NW, Washington, DC 20520
(202) 647-4000
Web site: www.state.gov

The bureau deals with U.S. foreign policy and U.S. relations with the countries in the Middle East, including Iraq. Its Web site offers country information as well as news briefings and press statements on U.S. foreign policy.

Washington Institute for Near East Policy
1828 L St. NW, Suite 1050, Washington, DC 20036
(202) 452-0650 • fax: (202) 223-5364
e-mail: info@washingtoninstitute.org
Web site: www.washingtoninstitute.org

The institute is an independent, nonprofit research organization that provides information and analysis on the Middle East and U.S. policy in the region. It publishes numerous books including *How to Build a New Iraq After Saddam*, as well as policy papers and reports on regional politics, security, and economics. Its Web site includes a special "Focus on Iraq" section that features articles and reports about that nation.

Bibliography

Books

Gilbert Archar	*The Clash of Barbarisms: September 11 and the Making of the New World Disorder.* New York: Monthly Review Press, 2002.
Joseph Braude	*The New Iraq: Rebuilding the Country for Its People, the Middle East, and the World.* New York: Basic Books, 2003.
Richard A. Clarke	*Against All Enemies: Inside America's War on Terror.* Detroit: Free Press, 2004.
Patrick Clawson, ed.	*How to Build a New Iraq After Saddam.* Washington, DC: Washington Institute for Near East Policy, 2002.
Toby Dodge and Steven Simon, eds.	*Iraq at the Crossroads: State and Society in the Shadow of Regime Change.* New York: Oxford University Press, 2003.
John L. Esposito and John O. Voll, eds.	*Islam and Democracy.* New York: Oxford University Press, 1996.
Deborah J. Gerner, ed.	*Understanding the Contemporary Middle East.* Boulder, CO: Lynne Reinner, 2000.
Dilip Hiro	*Iraq: In the Eye of the Storm.* New York: Thunder's Mouth Press, 2002.
Christopher Hitchens	*A Long Short War: The Postponed Liberation of Iraq.* New York: Plume, 2003.
Albert Hourani	*A History of the Arab Peoples.* Boston: Harvard University Press, 1997.
Lawrence F. Kaplan and William Kristol	*The War over Iraq: Saddam's Tyranny and America's Mission.* San Francisco: Encounter Books, 2003.
David W. Lesch, ed.	*The Middle East and the United States: A Historical and Political Reassessment.* Boulder, CO: Westview, 2003.
Bernard Lewis	*What Went Wrong: The Clash Between Islam and Modernity in the Middle East.* New York: HarperPerennial, 2003.
Sandra Mackey	*The Reckoning: Iraq and the Legacy of Saddam Hussein.* New York: W.W. Norton, 2002.
Norman Mailer	*Why Are We at War?* New York: Random House, 2003.
Kenneth M. Pollack	*The Threatening Storm: The Case for Invading Iraq.* New York: Random House, 2002.
Milan Rai	*War Plan Iraq: Ten Reasons Against War with Iraq.* New York: Verso, 2002.

Scott Ritter   *Endgame: Solving the Iraq Crisis.* New York: Simon & Schuster, 2002.

Micah L. Sifry and   *The Iraq War Reader: History, Documents, Opinions.* New Christopher Cerf, eds.   York: Touchstone Books, 2003.

Norman Soloman et al. *Target Iraq: What the News Media Didn't Tell You.* New York: Context Books, 2003.

Harlan Ullman   *Unfinished Business: Afghanistan, the Middle East and Beyond—Defusing the Dangers That Threaten American Security.* New York: Citadel Press, 2002.

Bob Woodward   *Plan of Attack.* New York: Simon & Schuster, 2004.

Periodicals

Spencer Ackerman   "The First Casualty: The Selling of the Iraq War," *New* and John B. Judis   *Republic*, June 30, 2003.

Mohammed Aldouri   "Iraq States Its Case," *New York Times*, October 17, 2002.

Frederick D. Barton   "Winning the Peace in Iraq," *Washington Quarterly*, and Bathsheba Crocker Spring 2003.

Russell Berman et al.   "The Dilemma of Reforming a Post-Saddam Iraq," *Commentary*, May 2003.

Carl Bildt   "Hard-Earned Lessons on Nation-Building: Seven Ways to Rebuild Iraq," *International Herald Tribune*, May 7, 2003.

David Brooks   "Building Democracy Out of What?" *Atlantic Monthly*, June 2003.

Phillip J. Brown   "Justice, Law, and War," *America*, August 18, 2003.

Juan Cole   "Questions of Peace and Genocide," *Tikkun*, May/June 2003.

Charles Colson   "Just War in Iraq: Sometimes Going to War Is the Charitable Thing to Do," *Christianity Today*, December 9, 2002.

Adeed I. Dawisha   "How to Build a Democratic Iraq," *Foreign Affairs*, and Karen Dawisha   May/June 2003.

Economist   "The Hard Path to New Nationhood: Rebuilding Iraq," April 16, 2003.

Thomas R. Eddlem   "War Under False Pretense," *New American*, August 11, 2003.

Bilal El-Amine   "Gunboat Democracy," *Left Turn*, May/June 2003.

Reuel Marc Gerecht   "A Necessary War," *Weekly Standard*, October 21, 2002.

John Gray   "Unfit for the Burdens of Empire," *New Statesman*, April 21, 2003.

Efraim Karsh   "Making Iraq Safe for Democracy," *Commentary*, April 2003.

Bill Keller   "The Boys Who Cried Wolfowitz," *New York Times*, June 14, 2003.

Michael T. Klare   "It's the Oil, Stupid," *Nation*, May 12, 2003.

Joe Klein   "To Remake Iraq, Invite the Neighbors Over," *Time*, May 5, 2003.

Dennis Kucinich   "The Bloodstained Path," *Progressive*, November 2002.

Jim Lacey   "Hide and Seek . . . and Seek: Where'd Those Weapons of Mass Destruction Get To?" *National Review*, June 16, 2003.

Edward N. Luttwak   "Democracy in Iraq? It's a Fairy Tale," *Los Angeles Times*, May 31, 2003.

National Review   "Weapons of Mass Destruction: Deceptions About Deceptions," July 14, 2003.

New York Times   "A Bigger U.N. Role in Iraq," September 4, 2003.

Martin Peretz   "Minority Rule—Who Shouldn't Run Iraq," *New Republic*, April 21, 2003.

Milton Viorst   "Iraq: Why They Don't Want Democracy," *Los Angeles Times*, May 25, 2003.

Fareed Zakaria   "What We Should Do Now," *Newsweek*, September 1, 2003.

Index